FIND HAPPINESS THROUGH
NEGATIVE THINKING

LARRY GOTTERER

Find Happiness through Negative Thinking

Copyright © 2021, Larry Gotterer. All rights reserved.

No part of this book may be reproduced or transmitted in any form or by any means, electronic or mechanical, including photocopying, recording, or by any information storage and retrieval system, without written permission from the author, except in the case of quotations in critical articles or reviews. No liability is assumed with respect to the use of the information contained herein, nor is any liability assumed for damages resulting from the use of information contained herein.

First Edition: April 2021

Library of Congress Control Number: 2021900998

ISBN: 978-1-7365006-0-6 (paperback)
ISBN: 978-1-7365006-1-3 (e-book)

Published in Boynton Beach, Florida
Printed in the United States of America

For more information, please contact:
larrygotterer@gmail.com

Disclaimer: This publication is sold with the understanding that the author is not engaged in rendering psychological, medical, or other professional health services. It contains the entertaining opinions, ideas, thoughts, and attitudes of its author and is not intended to provide helpful, useful, or even proven information on any subject covered. If expert assistance or counseling is needed, the services of a competent health care or mental health professional should be sought out.

The author and publisher specifically disclaim any responsibility for any liability, loss, or risk, personal or otherwise, which is incurred as a consequence, directly or indirectly, of the use and application of any of the contents of this book.

Dedications

To my loving wife, Luanne, whom I thought the world of even though I don't think much of the world. Rest in peace, sweetie.

To my mom and dad, who've shown endless love and support despite my denying their decades-long request for a DNA test.

To my son, Adam, who never once gave me reason to believe he'd be the kind of kid who killed his parents in the middle of the night as they slept.

To my girlfriend, Cindy, who is so positive she can't see how negative I am.

LEGAL MUMBO JUMBO

This book has not been approved by the AMA, CDC, HHS, FDA, EMA, WHO, or any other legitimate, illegitimate, recognized, or unrecognized organization with or without a catchy acronym, nor will it ever be.

All views, opinions, claims, and unfounded assertions in this literary opus are those of the author alone. They are not intended to serve as medical advice such as what you would receive at hospitals, clinics, or doctors' offices. This includes health care facilities with high mortality rates that would scare the living daylights out of anyone in pain.

You will require far superior support than the contents herein provide if you have been diagnosed with any medical condition, disorder, affliction, ailment, or illness—whether major, minor, or a medley. In this case consult a competent health care professional with multiple licenses, certifications, and degrees. The writer only possesses a driver's license, certificate of automobile insurance, and 98.6 degrees in body temperature.

By reading, scanning, or flipping through this treasure trove of questionable insights, you agree to hold the author harmless from any consequences—whether emotional, physical, imaginary, hallucinatory, or hypochondriacal. This is justified, as speculative logic indicates a high probability you were already dealing with preexisting, inherited, or psychosis-related conditions prior to purchasing, borrowing, or stealing this book.

Should you not comprehend the details of this disclaimer, please consult an attorney, law school student, or confidante who watches tons of TV legal dramas.

TABLE OF CONTENTS

Whom Can This Book Help?		ix
Chapter 1	Negativity Begins at Birth	1
Chapter 2	Negative Thinking Is a Powerful Weapon	8
Chapter 3	Half Full versus Half Empty	14
Chapter 4	You Gotta Have Faith…or Do You?	20
Chapter 5	Proof That Negativity Is Healthy	27
Chapter 6	Happily Never After	33
Chapter 7	There's Nothing Great about Great	39
Chapter 8	Wreck Your Day the Right Way	45
Chapter 9	Don't Believe It	51
Chapter 10	Get into Doubt	57
Chapter 11	~~XXXX XXXXX XX XXXXXXX~~	63
Chapter 12	Blame Yourself	65
Chapter 13	No Luck Is the Best Luck	71
Chapter 14	Don't Put off Procrastination	77
Chapter 15	It's Critical to Be Critical	83
Chapter 16	Playing Dumb Isn't Being Stupid	89
Chapter 17	Succeed at Failure	95

Chapter 18	Gripe, Grumble, Bitch, Bellyache, and Kvetch	101
Chapter 19	Be a Brave Worrier	107
Chapter 20	Don't Underestimate Underachieving	113
Chapter 21	Know Motivation	119
Chapter 22	Impatience Is the Virtue	123
Chapter 23	Hit Them Right between the Lies	129
Chapter 24	You Have My Sympathy	135
Chapter 25	Manage Anger like a Vampire	141
Chapter 26	Stop Making Excuses for Making Excuses	147
Chapter 27	You Want Your Back against the Wall	153
Chapter 28	Shrink Your Confidence without a Shrink	158
Chapter 29	Assume the Negative Position	164
Chapter 30	Surviving in the Screw Youniverse	170
Chapter 31	The Problem with Problems	176
Chapter 32	Be an Imperfectionist	182
Chapter 33	Mist Understandings	188
Chapter 34	Play All the Negative Angles	194
Chapter 35	Look on the Blah Side	200
Chapter 36	The Bitter End	206
Your Negativity Scale Score		212
Handy Negative Terms		214
Acknowledgments		217
About the Author		218
References		219
Notes		221

WHOM CAN THIS BOOK HELP?

- **Happy people** sensible enough to know it's only a matter of time before they will be as miserable as everyone else
- **Emotional people** who are experiencing as many ups and downs as stairs but are always out of step with life
- **Impatient people** unable to stay focused long enough to finish a senten
- **Clueless people** who are desperate to flee the planet Oblivion but can't find a return flight
- **Suspicious people** struggling with knowing everyone is out to get them and it's not a delusion
- **Crabby people** seeking to control their irritability without meditation or reducing caffeine and alcohol intake for fear it will make them even crankier
- **Obnoxious people** who are so annoying they can't stand themselves
- **Dejected people** curious about exploring how combining strong antidepressants with a powerful antipositive attitude will work
- **And you**

- 1 -

NEGATIVITY BEGINS AT BIRTH

Billions of babies have entered the world crying. We just got here, for God's sake! Are we already unhappy? Is it because womb service was suddenly discontinued after that big water leak? There are babies born who don't shed a tear. What happens to them? The doctor makes them cry too. But wait, a birth is supposed to be a happy time. Why arrive crying?

Obstetricians tell us that crying is a good sign the baby's lungs are functioning. The real question is: Why don't we enter laughing, which also stimulates the lungs and heart while increasing oxygen intake? It's a clear-cut clue, which is impossible to say ten times fast, verifying the connection to negativity at birth. From our first breaths, we all start out as damn crybabies.

Another negative is the majority of us arrive via vaginal delivery. This makes the average person uneasy. Next time you're asked, "Where are you from?" see what kind of reaction you get by answering, "A vagina." Even though umpteen of us hail from one, hardly anyone wishes to declare it. Adults stay in their comfort zones with answers like "Cleveland" as opposed to "West Vagina." In Venice, Italy—known for its mother lode of canals—it's nearly impossible to find a gondolier propelling his oar through the water while offering views of a birth canal.

Giving birth can be long, painful, stressful, and laborious for women. All negatives. Little-known locker-room reports reveal that men also experience adverse side effects and psychological pressures connected to their births later in life. Long after their own vaginal deliveries, a significant percentage of males struggle to discern why it takes babies about forty weeks to make it out of a vagina but what can feel like an eternity as an adult to get back into one.

On one hand the frustration for an untold number of men is compounded by the sheer volume of options. Any vagina except for the original is desirable, yet the rejection rate far outpaces the ejaculation rate. On the other hand, well, that's why there is the other hand. The same report reveals that women who are negatively affected by a vaginal drought of sexual activity achieve satisfaction simply by watching a full season of *The Bachelor*.

Another shocking statistic is the tally of boys and girls who find traveling the Vaginaduct so stressful, they develop a form of vagiphobia. This may explain why masses of them grow up to be more anal than others.

A meaningful number of babies take a different route, bypassing the vagina altogether and pushing for C-sections. Long-term potential issues can follow, negatively affecting a baby's mental state for life. For instance, renowned comedian and life philosopher Steven Wright admits, "I was born by caesarean section, but you really can't tell...except that when I leave my house, I always go out the window."

It's unheard of for this to happen with any other kind of delivery—from natural or unnatural to Amazon Prime. Two other negative drawbacks of caesarean births are they can leave the mom scarred and trigger bikini stress syndrome.

Regardless of delivery method, the birth of a child is considered a cause for celebration by both optimists and pessimists. Of course the degree of festivity depends on how much of the Neanderthal gene the offspring inherited.

Perception is deceptive as well. Peering through the window of the baby nursery, unsuspecting parents, relatives, and friends only see the positives. No one knows whether baby Arlo will aspire to be a pharmacist or a drug dealer...or if tiny Tallulah will eventually run a business or a Ponzi scheme...or whether little Dick will become a PR director or a porn star. The newborn may be floating in three ounces of drool, have a conehead, and look like Yoda, yet the family's support team will swear under oath they have the most beautiful or handsome and gifted baby of all. As you will learn in subsequent chapters, this isn't the way real life progresses for people like you.

After birth there is also afterbirth—the name of the placental and fetal membrane expulsion that follows folks out of the birth canal. A growing number of women are eating their placentas as part of the childbirth experience. Meanwhile most dads are perfectly content with an alcoholic beverage or a cigar. What would make a mom want to eat her placenta? It turns out there is more to this practice than trying to find an alternative to horrible hospital food.

In his blog post, "Placenta: To Eat or Not to Eat," Mark B. Kristal, behavioral neuroscientist and professor in the Department of Psychology at the University of Buffalo, points out that women are eating placentas raw, cooked, blended into smoothies, or dried and encapsulated. Kristal claims women do this to prevent or reduce negative effects of childbirth such as postpartum depression, "baby blues," fatigue, lactational insufficiency, and hormone deficiencies.[1]

This trend serves as further evidence supporting the underlying conception of negativity starting at birth. If you think prepregnancy cravings for pickles and ice cream are a treat, wait until you try a postpartum placenta pepperoni pizza. There are obstetricians who warn that placenta eating can be harmful to moms and their babies. Make sure to consult a nutritionist who has studied the differences between fetus and feed us as they relate to placenta menus.

It's clear from birth that life is not meant to be an easy or necessarily positive journey. You come out bald, drooling, toothless, unable to talk or walk, and can't stop number one-ing and number two-ing all over yourself. If you live long enough, it's how your life might end too. Fun times.

Woo-hoo! This is only day one.

How much weight does your negativity scale hold?

Answer the mindset measurers after each chapter and keep track of your score. At the end of the final chapter, see what your total points reveal on pages 212 to 213. If you're reading the e-book version, use a separate sheet of paper and do not attempt to write on your device screen.

Negativity Scale Checkpoint

Chapter 1: Negativity Begins at Birth

1. From what I recall of my birth, the movie title that offers an accurate sneak preview of my arrival is…

    a) *A Star Is Born* _____ (5 Points)
    b) *Boss Baby* _____ (10 Points)
    c) *Dazed and Confused* _____ (15 Points)
    d) *Parasite* _____ (20 Points)

2. The image a vagina brings to mind for me is…

    a) The holy grail _____ (5 Points)
    b) A hot, buttered roll _____ (10 Points)
    c) A revolving door _____ (15 Points)
    d) A forest without trees _____ (20 Points)

3. The moment my parents laid eyes on me, they said something like…

    a) "You're so adorable!" _____ (5 Points)
    b) "Goochie goochie goo!" _____ (10 Points)
    c) "Do they take trade-ins?" _____ (15 Points)
    d) "WTF!" _____ (20 Points)

4. On my first birthday, if a profiler from the FBI observed me, they'd see right away I was on the fast track to becoming a bona fide…

    a) Conformist _____ (5 Points)
    b) Reformist _____ (10 Points)
    c) Alarmist _____ (15 Points)
    d) Contortionist _____ (20 Points)

5. **Revealing whether my mother did or didn't eat her placenta is a violation of HIPAA. I can say I'm the way I am because she's the kind of person who would...**

    a) Read everything about eating placentas before doing anything   _____ (5 Points)
    b) Ask everyone she knows whether they've eaten a placenta and do what the majority did   _____ (10 Points)
    c) Procrastinate too long and do nothing, while preserving her placenta in the freezer   _____ (15 Points)
    d) Not care and go through life never knowing what a placenta is   _____ (20 Points)

Total Points, Chapter 1   _____

Gotterer's Theory of Negativity

$$N = WCS^{(100°)} \times S/P$$

Negativity equals worst-case scenario
(to the one hundredth degree)
times stress over panic.

-2-

NEGATIVE THINKING IS A POWERFUL WEAPON

Negativity isn't only for pessimists. It's for your own good. What about optimists? If you've been burned so often by what you want to happen not happening, you can stop covering your positive-thinking, thick skin in aloe vera. Soothing relief awaits.

The downside of positivity is that it's frequently disguised. Long, red, flowing hair halfway down someone's back catches the attention of a man at a bar. He's excited by the possibilities. In his mind he's going home with her. As he approaches, the person turns. It's a guy with a long beard and a cold sore. So much for positive thinking. Such beautiful, soft, shiny hair too.

What appears positive doesn't guarantee favorable outcomes. Here's a shocker: negativity can generate positive results. There are times you move forward but land backward. Other times you step backward to push forward. Plenty of times you go sideways. At times you're running around in circles. From time to time, you move forward and backward simultaneously, which if you do too rapidly can rupture your coccyx. Negative thinking merges all of these times into an all-the-time solution for whatever direction you're going.

There is more to negativity than declaring, "That sucks!" or "I hate it." You may not have been a fan of negative thinking in the past; however, it has adapted to keep pace with the skyrocketing rise of incompetency, indecency, and insanity. Plus present principles, practices, perceptions, patterns, and persuasions of pessimism progressed purposefully over centuries. They are based on ongoing, in-depth observation of large groups consisting of chronic complainers, nonstop nitpickers, experts in feeling or giving guilt, distinguished members of Dissenters, Disapprovers, Deplorers, Decriers, & Denouncers Unlimited, toxic mothers-in-law, and impossible-to-please princesses from Long Island.

Undocumented studies conducted by medical professionals spanning six thousand years reveal that optimists experience astronomically high levels of acid reflux, angina, cortisol, and dark-green bile when their hopes for the best don't materialize. By becoming proficient in negativity, you'll soon develop enviable capabilities that protect your central nervous system from any spouse, partner, ex, relative, neighbor, coworker, pet, stranger, insect, nonliving object, or figment of your imagination.

You've been taught to think positively your whole life. Why is now the time to change course and go negative? Deep down you know. That's why you bought a book called *Find Happiness through Negative Thinking*. The world is changing, and for legions of its inhabitants, it's not looking good. Turn on the news and see how many stories make you feel hopeless instead of hopeful. Based on overwhelming feedback from focus groups of suburban moms exiting supermarkets in Iowa, rumor has it CBS is bringing back the popular soap opera *As the World Turns* under the new name *As the World Turns Your Stomach*.

Texts, tweets, and posts have replaced conversations. Greed, corruption, and arrogance are as rampant as roaches in inner-city restaurants. Backstabbing has become a more popular sport than ice hockey, and it's easier to learn if you have weak ankles. Requests for shoving various objects up your rear orifice are at an all-time high. So are surgical procedures for removing them. And have a nice day!

Positive thinking lost its edge. Bounteous numbers of high hopes and promises have been left unfulfilled. Focusing on the negative protects you when things don't work out, which is most of the time. You'll develop instincts and intuition to insulate yourself from optimistic blowhards who gush positive, pie-in-the-sky nonsense and believe they can turn lemonade back into lemons. Don't fall for their deceptive inspirations either, like "When life tastes like dry cat food, have faith and your salivation will come" or "When life hands you crap, make do."

Where and when do you use negative thinking? Everywhere you go, twenty-four hours a day, if not longer when factoring in time zone changes and leap years. You should even dream in the negative, whether it's one dream or you're binge watching.

Positive thinkers hope for the best. They hope they'll get the job. They hope their team takes the championship. They hope to win the lottery. Hope repeatedly leaves them deflated or crushed, like a fiancé left standing at the altar after his bride-to-be discovers the bite on his neck wasn't from a spider.

Negative thinkers expect the worst. They're convinced there's no way they're getting the job. They don't expect their team to win anything. They know there's no chance they'll pick the lottery numbers that hit. As a result they're not defeated when things don't work out. They expected it all along. If something good happens, they're still ecstatic.

Impatience is imperative as you embark on your negative journey. Progress then accelerates. When can you expect results? Almost immediately once you integrate each chapter's pessimistic pointers into your minute-to-minute mindset. Like any worthwhile skill, mastering the influence of negative thinking won't happen overnight. Family and friends will say, "Stay positive; things will turn around." Yeah, and the Messiah should be here any day now.

The present sucks for millions of us. We're entering a new era in which disappointment spreads faster than the rate of germs breeding on gas pump handles. The solution is to negatize your attitudes and actions into an effective weapon for finding happiness. As an added bonus, you'll earn the right to say something masses of mortals cannot say—that you read a book.

Negativity Scale Checkpoint

Chapter 2: Negative Thinking Is a Powerful Weapon

1. My current arsenal of negativity is the equivalent of…

    a) A pesky peashooter _____ (5 Points)
    b) A splashy Super Soaker _____ (10 Points)
    c) A constant attack drone _____ (15 Points)
    d) An I-might-go-ballistic missile _____ (20 Points)

2. When I dish out a taste of negativity, it's seasoned with my…

    a) Whine and cheesy personality _____ (5 Points)
    b) Salt-and-vinegar, chippy boldness _____ (10 Points)
    c) Sweet and sourpuss sarcasm _____ (15 Points)
    d) Hot-and-spicy, saucy temper _____ (20 Points)

3. If I had a universal remote to control my world, the button I'd wear out first is…

    a) Fast-forward _____ (5 Points)
    b) Pause _____ (10 Points)
    c) Mute _____ (15 Points)
    d) Rewind _____ (20 Points)

4. I find myself in real-life situations with the kind of characters you'd see on…

    a) *Friends* _____ (5 Points)
    b) *Unsolved Mysteries* _____ (10 Points)
    c) *Arrested Development* _____ (15 Points)
    d) *The Walking Dead* _____ (20 Points)

5. **Once things turn for the worse, my strategy is...**

    a) Listen, fix, relax, move on   _____ (5 Points)
    b) Sigh, stare, fidget, cringe   _____ (10 Points)
    c) Run, hide, sulk, sleep   _____ (15 Points)
    d) Rant, stomp, curse, repeat   _____ (20 Points)

Total Points, Chapter 2   _____

Prepare for the worst or
at least the best of the worst.

-3-

HALF FULL VERSUS HALF EMPTY

Between wearing glasses and drinking from them, it can get confusing. One kind you see with but don't drink from. The other kind you drink from but don't see with, although there is one unique view drinking glasses provide that's crystal clear.

It is a transparent, psychological, glass-half-full-or-half-empty theory to see if you're an optimist or a pessimist. Thankfully they had the foresight not to develop this test with eyeglasses. Sorting out who's positive and who's negative based on who's half sighted and who's half blind would be a who's-who nightmare. Complications would have compromised the procedure, arising from glass eyes and blind studies alone.

The glass-half-full-or-half-empty theory doesn't hold water anyway. It only tells half the story. We're taught this balderdash by parents, even though their kids swear they never want to be like them when they grow up, out-of-shape coaches who've never won anything, teachers who are part of an education system that gets an F for fiasco, and therapists who may be in therapy themselves.

Why does anyone of alleged sound mind buy into this glass-half-full drivel—and in some cases dribble? The success rate of its presenters is iffy at best. In the human race, hordes of beings don't even win, place, or show.

What's wrong with seeing the glass as half empty when it is equally half full? This warrants a closer look. Let's analyze it with semiscientific evidence strongly supported by convincing hearsay.

Try this eye-opening experiment:

Step 1: Employ two volunteers. Don't go as far as offering them a staff position, salary, and benefits. One should be a half full fan, the other a half empty believer. There's a possibility this endeavor may irk the half full participant. Your half empty guest won't care; they've already run through and accepted all worst-case scenarios.

Step 2: Find two identical glasses and position them side by side. In this case identical means size and shape. If one glass is scratched, it isn't necessary to scratch the other in the exact same place. This level of identicalness may please obsessive-compulsive participants but will have no impact whatsoever on the final results.

Advisory: If you're looking at these glasses without your glasses and can't see anything, change all further references in this chapter about glasses to cups.
Disclaimer: The outcome of this experiment using cups won't be nearly as accurate. They are deceiving and have a tendency to runneth over.

Step 3: Fill both glasses precisely to the halfway point with a liquid that isn't scorching hot or ice cold. Aim for a comfortable room temperature as long as you're not in a room such as a sauna or mortuary cold chamber.

Step 4: For argument's sake let's say the glass on the left is half full and the glass on the right is half empty. If you disagree, reverse them. This experiment is foolproof and works either way. Now pour the half full glass over the head of the half empty supporter.

Step 5: Spill the half empty glass over the head of the half full volunteer. If they cry remind them it's not milk and no one cries over spilled water. Who got more wet?

Technically they both got the same amount of wet since the volume of water in each glass was identical. Still, given the choice, wouldn't you psychologically feel less wet if the glass dumped over your head were half empty instead of half full?

Aren't you more likely to take out the trash if it is half full than half empty? This explains why positive people take out the trash way more often than pessimists. Negative folks don't care; it's only half empty. Who has time to keep taking out half empty trash all day long?

If you accidentally fell into a snake pit, wouldn't you be praying the pit was half empty of snakes? Half full sounds like a lot more snakes. For that matter, if you're an optimist, how in the world did you fall into a snake pit?

Why did the visionaries who dreamed this up only see the glass as half full? Liquids don't even cost much. They could have easily filled the entire glass for fractions of a penny and told everyone to see it as all the way full. Why even bother to entertain the level of liquid in a glass at all? Someone who's dehydrated is not going to care one bit how full or empty the glass is, even if they're fully or half fully dehydrated.

It's the same thing with shit. Everyone agrees someone can be full of shit. No one ever accuses anyone of being half full of shit unless it's due to a poor colonoscopy prep. This is indisputable proof of why the entire glass-half-full concept is also half assed.

Now would be a good time to absorb what you've learned and take a water break, unless you're pregnant.

Negativity Scale Checkpoint

Chapter 3: Half Full versus Half Empty

1. **My chances of conducting this glass-half-full-or-half-empty experiment is best expressed by…**

    a) "Are you nuts?" _____ (5 Points)
    b) "My friends would have me committed!" _____ (10 Points)
    c) "Maybe, maybe not." _____ (15 Points)
    d) "I'm going to pour water on heads by the gallon!" _____ (20 Points)

2. **Family and friends who know me well would say I'm the one who's…**

    a) Never full of bull _____ (5 Points)
    b) Running on empty _____ (10 Points)
    c) Always coming up empty-handed _____ (15 Points)
    d) Not playing with a full deck _____ (20 Points)

3. **Since the first day of my life, I've had…**

    a) More positively positive days _____ (5 Points)
    b) More negatively positive days _____ (10 Points)
    c) More positively negative days _____ (15 Points)
    d) More negatively negative days _____ (20 Points)

4. **After analyzing myself in terms of half, there's a better chance I would…**

    a) Give someone half a chance _____ (5 Points)
    b) Do something half trying _____ (10 Points)
    c) Refuse to meet halfway _____ (15 Points)
    d) Go off half-cocked _____ (20 Points)

5. **If I had an imaginary glass to keep track of all the things I fully agreed with, half agreed with, half disagreed with, and fully disagreed with over the last six months, it would be...**

   a) Full of agreed   _____ (5 Points)
   b) Half full of agreed   _____ (10 Points)
   c) Half empty of disagreed   _____ (15 Points)
   d) Full of disagreed   _____ (20 Points)

Total Points, Chapter 3   _____

It's better to be a happy pessimist
than an unhappy optimist.

-4-

YOU GOTTA HAVE FAITH... OR DO YOU?

It is widely believed that God created the heavens and the earth in six days and took a well-deserved personal day on the seventh. This is a mind-boggling accomplishment, considering after multiple decades our brightest minds still can't figure out how to rebuild Flint, Michigan.

To further put this world-class achievement into perspective, the Roman Empire let everyone know it would take time for Rome to be built. Italians all over Italy were *arrabbiato* when they learned it would take close to one thousand years. None of them had that much time to kill. Passing the days stuffing their faces with focaccia and osso buco only added to the weight put on their shoulders and the rest of their bodies.

Optimists tried to spin it to their advantage. To this day they say, "Rome wasn't built in a day," as if it's a good thing. Negative thinkers interpreted the expression as nothing more than a stalling tactic used to cover up false promises, delays, negligence, and incompetence.

After God created this beautiful world, why did He stick negative elements into it? Light, sky, land, seas, plants, trees, sun, moon, stars, locusts, tsunamis, ingrown toenails, lice, bowel obstructions...the answer is obvious: no one understood the strength of negativity better than the

Lord. Once you've survived a plague, you'll never take feeling healthy for granted. The outdoors forever look more heavenly after you've been attacked by a swarm of Africanized killer bees. You need to get hit by a car moving at a minimum of forty-five miles per hour to feel anything more excruciating than a kidney stone. After you do you'll appreciate being pain free like never before.

God didn't stop there. Take the Ten Commandments—arguably the most intimidating list of moral instructions ever written to base one's life on. It's not possible to write this type of messaging in the affirmative and get anyone to obey.

Next thing you know, Moses, and subsequently Charlton Heston, are schlepping around two tablets in 128-degree Middle Eastern heat heavy enough to give both of them double hernias. God could have said, "Let there be paper," jotted down His commands, and called it a day. But no! Making the commandments as threateningly negative as possible—and writing them in stone—is what gave them oomph. Let's examine a few life-changing examples so almighty they'll have you shouting, "Oh, Lordy!"

"Thou shalt have no other gods before Me."

Translation: "I'm the only god you need, and remember: the concept of striking people with lightning is mine." Try to spin this commandment in a positive light. Who in God's name is going to obey, "Out of all gods, please make me your go-to god"? His negative tone is so strong, people centuries later still don't put other gods before Him or even after Him, and He didn't even mention anything about that.

Key Negative Takeaway: Put "no" on your list of favorite words. Don't hesitate to be a no it all.

"Thou shalt not take the name of the Lord thy God in vain."

Translation: "Use My name without expressed written consent, and I will kick your butt from here to kingdom come." Religious insiders are rumored to affirm He finds "OMG" especially irritating. The commandment loses its pow when positively altered to, "Please respect My name and do Me a favor: keep the blasphemy to a minimum."

Key Negative Takeaway: Use "not" a lot. Greater results and respect follow once you tie people up in nots.

"Thou shalt not covet thy neighbor's house; thou shalt not covet thy neighbor's wife, nor his manservant, nor his maidservant, nor his ox, nor his ass, nor his donkey, nor any thing that is thy neighbor's."

Translation: "Stay away from the folks next door and get your own pets to play with." The series of "nor" in this commandment effectively struck fear throughout neighborhoods everywhere. It didn't take long for residents to find a loophole. God never mentioned anything about not coveting those things if they weren't thy neighbor's. Before you could blink, sneaking off to covet them in other communities caught on. Either way, anyone who would covet the donkey next door—or even one living within driving distance—has serious issues. At least with a neighbor's ass, there's a defense for it—depending on what the ass looks like.

Key Negative Takeaway: For maximum effect, be sure to scatter the word "nor" at least five to eight times in a sentence like He did.

God knew what He was doing. "Thou shalt not kill" would surely outlive "Thou shalt make best efforts to keep those thy encounter alive."

"Thou shalt not steal" is way more enforceable than "Thou shalt avoid bypassing the checkout counter before running out of the store with merchandise."

"Thou shalt not commit adultery" is much less likely to be cheated on than "Thou shalt only fantasize about adultery but stop short of committing it."

The Ten Commandments worked because they are the ultimate in negative thinking for living the right way. Don't take my word for it; take God's.

Alternatively, adopting a positive approach can lead to misunderstood interpretations with unexpected results. For example suicide bombers believe they will go to heaven, where seventy-two virgins await. It's hard to get more positive than that. Yet according to a Global Nation report, Canadian author and Quran scholar Irshad Manji said on a CNN special show called *Why They Hate Us* that the word "virgin" in the Quran meant "raisin." [2] Receiving seventy-two raisins upon arrival instead of virgins is sure to surprise swarms of new martyrs.

Furthermore, an unheard-of study no one reported reveals that a majority of devoted religious followers from all faiths will do anything their god asks for free. A compelling, sizably smaller percent confess that depending on the size of the request, they would try to hold out for at least a Virgin Mary and a medium-sized trophy.

Everyone knows where they negatively stand with the Ten Commandments. Whether you believe in a god or not, there is no doubt that negative thinking carries a higher power.

Negativity Scale Checkpoint

Chapter 4: You Gotta Have Faith...or Do You?

1. The song title most in tune with my philosophy as it pertains to believing is...

    a) "I'm a Believer" _____ (5 Points)
    b) "Believe in Yourself" _____ (10 Points)
    c) "What a Fool Believes" _____ (15 Points)
    d) "Don't Believe a Word" _____ (20 Points)

2. Aside from whatever sins I've committed, I'm also guilty of breaking more...

    a) Dishes _____ (5 Points)
    b) Promises _____ (10 Points)
    c) Bones _____ (15 Points)
    d) Laws _____ (20 Points)

3. I'm convinced the last miracle I witnessed was performed by...

    a) A higher power _____ (5 Points)
    b) A mere mortal _____ (10 Points)
    c) An alien force _____ (15 Points)
    d) David Copperfield _____ (20 Points)

4. In my opinion, the Ten Commandments are...

    a) Negative but positive _____ (5 Points)
    b) Positive but negative _____ (10 Points)
    c) Overkill _____ (15 Points)
    d) A bluff _____ (20 Points)

5. **The last time God spoke to me directly was…**

    a) Earlier today   _____ (5 Points)
    b) Within the last few weeks   _____ (10 Points)
    c) Months or years ago   _____ (15 Points)
    d) He clearly lost my number   _____ (20 Points)

Total Points, Chapter 4   _____

You can learn more by turning a
single positive into a double negative.

-5-

PROOF THAT NEGATIVITY IS HEALTHY

There are countless reasons to think negatively in terms of your health. Name one lab test result you want to come back positive. See? The foundation of the entire medical profession is based on praying, hoping, or wishing for negative results.

You can argue there is one exception to this rule—a pregnancy test—and you'd lose the argument. Pregnancy tests don't count since a positive result is considered negative when a couple would have preferred scrambled eggs and ham over fertilized egg and sperm. Once the baby is born, it's not always positive either. After all, how many children have you met who had you saying, "I feel sorry for that kid's parents"?

Speaking of parents, they offer terrific negative-driven health advice. Moms are famous for preventative and protective wisdom such as "Put on a coat or you'll catch pneumonia!" or "Put that down before you poke an eye out!" Mom's approach is dead-on. If pneumonia doesn't happen, or an eyeball doesn't pop out of its socket, no harm done. In a bad or worst-case scenario, you were warned of the risks and can't say it caught you by surprise. This proves that negative moms are onto something. Look back on your childhood, and you'll have all the evidence you need. How many one-eyed, coatless friends did you have who caught pneumonia every time it got cold out?

Thanks to positive thinking, the unhealthy aren't honest about how they feel anymore. If someone asks, "How are you feeling?" you'll hear a generic, positive, short reply like "Fine" or "Pretty good" or "Great!" Here's where you can learn a lot from Jewish people. Ask them how they feel, and you'll know on the spot if their backs are killing them, what their pooping schedules are, whether their hemorrhoids are on fire, how many stents they have, what surgery they're scheduled for, and how they almost died last week.

One word of caution: Don't take everything literally when listening to two or more Jews who are hard of hearing discuss their health. Conversations are often confusing.

"Her brother is a cantor?"

"No, he has cancer!"

"He's a tenor?"

"No, he's got a tumor!"

By the time the exchange is over, you can't tell if the brother is going to sing at a concert, have part of his liver removed, or eat chopped liver for lunch.

Letting people know you feel bad makes you feel better. Get any pain in the neck off your back, not just spinal stenosis. The other person feels better too. Compared to what you have, they'll happily live with what they've got.

The problem with being positive is you're not prepared when things go wrong, and you're left shattered when they do. Taking a negative approach is like getting a heads-up to counter the element of surprise. It also allows you to be surprised when it's not as bad as expected. Being negative doesn't mean you're destined for poor health. Hopeful marathon runners are not immune to heart attacks. Sanguine nonsmokers get lung cancer. Upbeat tourists in Mexico who drink bottled water don't escape Montezuma's revenge. Confident porn stars still suffer severe groin strains.

It's impossible to avoid annoyances like anxiety, acne, anger, aggravation, allergies, or abdominal pain forever, which is only the tip of the ailment iceberg. Treating a negative with a negative delivers additional relief without side effects like rashes, even while you're making rash decisions. When your body is under attack, strike back by ruminating on how much worse it could be.

Let's say you are having a panic attack. You're sweating profusely, the room is spinning, and your trachea is closed tighter than a jar lid an arthritic is trying to open. Visualize a scenario that makes you feel better. Put someone you dislike on a spaceship and send them on a one-way trip to Uranus, but not the planet. Or envision how much worse life would be if your debts were doubled…tripled…quadrupled. Owing $100,000, $150,000, or $200,000 makes owing $50,000 feel like lunch money. The good news is, this kind of debt never needs to be repaid.

Being positive won't make your physical or mental problems disappear. By developing skills to leverage a negative, mind-over-matter mindset, you'll soon sense how much worse your issues could be, which will make the ones you have seem less daunting.

It is difficult to feel healthy for long. The world is full of contagious crowds, infected surfaces, poisonous substances, and flesh-eating forces from bacteria to cannibals. People we meet on a daily basis are enough to make us sick.

You expect a negative result for everything for which the medical profession tests, other than possibly one indicating you're expecting. What more proof do you need that negativity is the healthiest way to go?

The title of comedian Bruce Smirnoff's award-winning one-man show says it best: *Other Than My Health I Have Nothing…and Today I Don't Feel So Good.*

Negativity Scale Checkpoint

Chapter 5: Proof That Negativity Is Healthy

1. When considering that the human body consists of up to 60 percent water, the amount of negativity flowing through my remaining percentage is…

    a) 0–10 percent   _____ (5 Points)
    b) 11–20 percent   _____ (10 Points)
    c) 21–30 percent   _____ (15 Points)
    d) 31–40 percent   _____ (20 Points)

2. When I awaken in the morning, I'm usually feeling…

    a) Happy   _____ (5 Points)
    b) Yappy   _____ (10 Points)
    c) Snappy   _____ (15 Points)
    d) Crappy   _____ (20 Points)

3. If brain fluid could be replaced by any other kind of flowing substance, the inside of my cranium would be soaking in…

    a) Honey   _____ (5 Points)
    b) Caffeinated coffee   _____ (10 Points)
    c) Brake fluid   _____ (15 Points)
    d) Liquid pain reliever _____ (20 Points)

4. I wish I could find a medical specialist to help me…

    a) Stop my mouth from running   _____ (5 Points)
    b) See past the end of my nose   _____ (10 Points)
    c) Prevent myself from getting cold feet _____ (15 Points)
    d) Develop thicker skin   _____ (20 Points)

5. **My overall well-being would improve immensely if I had less trouble clearing my...**

   a) Sinuses _____ (5 Points)
   b) Name _____ (10 Points)
   c) Conscience _____ (15 Points)
   d) Bad karma _____ (20 Points)

   Total Points, Chapter 5 _____

Once you replace positive thoughts with negative ones, you'll have more positive results.

-6-

HAPPILY NEVER AFTER

Everyone dreams of living happily ever after. What a crock of fictional, folkloric, fantasy-tale crap! There is no fairy godmother with magical mentoring powers you can speed dial. Ladies, forget about a prince knocking on your door with a lost glass slipper, high-priced Nike sneaker, or glittering, high-heeled Prada shoe. Guys, you might meet a queen, but it'll be more like a drama queen, drag queen, or worker at a Dairy Queen.

Happy endings are few and far between these days, unless you know an entrepreneurial masseuse. That reminds me of a trip I took to Bangkok back in the summer of—well, there's a whole other book. The point is you can be much happier living happily never after.

Being happy is hard work without a prescription. Everyone you know advises you to be well, be good, be your best, be a hard worker, be brave, be careful, be cool, be different, be grateful, be humble, be joyful, be kind, be positive, be patient, be responsible, and be safe. You can't be everything to everyone. Tell them all you want to be is left alone.

"Be yourself" is another peculiar piece of positive people encouragement. It doesn't apply to a large segment of society who you wish weren't themselves, including blabbermouths, ass kissers, ball breakers, never apologizers, jagoffs, finger snappers, and sidewalk spitters.

If you've tried not being yourself before, you didn't find any increased happiness there. Otherwise you'd still be one of the alternative people you tried being.

There are times you'll think, *I don't feel like myself today.* Whom do you feel like? Feeling like someone else never does anyone any good. It's like subletting your body to a complete stranger without collecting rent. Plus if that person doesn't dress like you, it'll cost you a bundle after they spring for a whole new wardrobe without your approval. Furthermore when you don't feel like yourself for an extended period of time, other things change such as your diet, car, job, boyfriend or girlfriend, husband or wife, and where you live. Once you feel like yourself again, what if you're locked out of your own home by whom you were feeling like?

There are thousands of books and studies about happiness. The people who wrote and researched them—and supposedly know everything there is to know about achieving happiness—aren't always happy.

When you wallow in negativity, you don't expect to be happy but appreciate it more when you are. Can you be happy and never find true love? Could you make a living as a thief if you believed it was an honest way to make a living? Are you able to accept that you're ugly but pretend it doesn't matter as long as the number of mirrors in your home is kept to a minimum? You're right; why would anyone say yes to any of that? The secret is accepting the hand you're dealt and taking happiness when you can get it, versus continuously expecting it and not achieving it.

The entire concept of happiness is unpredictable. Couples go separate ways and everyone they know speculates why.

"They seemed so happy."

Little do they know that for years she lay awake every night, hoping he'd stop breathing due to natural causes, so she wouldn't have to duct tape a pillow over his head and risk jail time. Meanwhile he dreamed of mixing maximum-strength rat poison into her tub of protein powder.

Singles galore feel dejected that they're not married. A multitude of committed couples are in the dumps about not being single. An army of working people are dismayed by their jobs. Slews of naked bodies are in distress over their stomachs, butts, breasts, or penis sizes. Positive thinking isn't helping any of them.

It's debatable whether money can buy happiness. Plenty of experts say it can't. Although in a secret survey of celebrities who've gone from rags to riches, back to rags, and then off to rehab, most agree that being rich is better than being poor, whether it makes them happier or not. While it's true there are unhappy rich people and happy poor people, it's not true that no one is happy about being unhappy. When you're happy about being unhappy, you're still happy about something. It's okay to feel unhappy enough to simmer down your expectations in case any happiness received reverts back to unhappiness.

There are three major problems with happiness:

1. It doesn't last.
2. It's temporary.
3. It is short lived.

Positive brainwashing over the years may have conditioned you to be fearful of anything negative. As a result you become unhappy at the first sign of something going wrong. This is where embracing negativity goes a long way. If you accept the inevitability of things going wrong—and sooner or later, they will—you won't freak out when they do. This allows you to make more rational decisions regarding how to proceed, which leads to increased happiness.

At the first unhappy notion of "this is bad," think, *Bad isn't as bad as worse*. After that, worse isn't nearly as bad as terrible. Then again terrible doesn't even come close to horrific. Of course horrific is a far cry from devastating. Certainly devastating is much more manageable than catastrophic. From there catastrophic means you can at least find consolation in knowing you can't feel any worse. You'll be glad you did and live happily never after.

Negativity Scale Checkpoint

Chapter 6: Happily Never After

1. The emotions associated with happiness flowing through my veins feel like...

   a) Gush, gush, gush   _____ (5 Points)
   b) Splash, splash, splash   _____ (10 Points)
   c) Squirt, squirt, squirt   _____ (15 Points)
   d) Drip, drip, drip   _____ (20 Points)

2. An appropriate title for my autobiography is...

   a) *Happier Than You*   _____ (5 Points)
   b) *Happy. Sad. Happy. Sad.*   _____ (10 Points)
   c) *Unhappy. Unlucky. Unfazed.*   _____ (15 Points)
   d) *Unhappier Than a Mime Who Stinks at Charades*   _____ (20 Points)

3. You will see the most evidence of happiness by looking deep into my...

   a) Soul   _____ (5 Points)
   b) Dreams   _____ (10 Points)
   c) Out-of-body experiences   _____ (15 Points)
   d) Weekly garbage   _____ (20 Points)

4. My level of happiness or unhappiness is directly related to my being so...

   a) Flawless   _____ (5 Points)
   b) Fearless   _____ (10 Points)
   c) Humorless   _____ (15 Points)
   d) Clueless   _____ (20 Points)

5. If a team of happyologists conducted a thorough happiness audit of my last three years, they would categorize me as…

   a) Super happy　　　　　　　　　_____ (5 Points)
   b) More happy than unhappy　　_____ (10 Points)
   c) Not happy or unhappy　　　　_____ (15 Points)
   d) Happily unhappy　　　　　　 _____ (20 Points)

   Total Points, Chapter 6　　　　_____

If at first you don't succeed,
cry, cry again.

〜

-7-

THERE'S NOTHING GREAT ABOUT GREAT

Optimists operate as if greatness is embedded in the purified air they walk on. All of them know a great pizza place or a great doctor and can endorse a great miracle cure for everything from snoring to sore nipples. Believing isn't enough for propagandists of greatness.

"Be a great believer," they preach. A good deal won't do. Hold out for a great deal. The outdoors is beautiful but nothing like the great outdoors. Regular strides don't cut it. Making progress happens with great strides. An average number of pains falls short. Go to great pains. Nothing is more satisfying than taking a great, big dump. Any dump used to be a joy, even if you needed to coax it out with a fiber supplement or enema. Now greatness is attached to dumps. Toilet bowl manufacturers are still playing catch-up, trying to invent a great flash-flood flush.

Polluting the planet with greatness needs to stop. Humans releasing positive emissions that go bad and contaminate the nozone layer are at fault. Negative energy offsets this cataclysmic bunk. The answer is to reduce extraordinarily high levels of greatness, which aren't sustainable.

Wean yourself off greatness by knocking down your expectations to negative goodness. Start with the basics—good grief, good riddance, won't do any good, good-for-nothing, and middle-finger-licking good.

Next advance to sucks—this sucks, that sucks, you suck, suck it up, and suck my succotash. Doesn't matter if you think it, say it, or feel it, the perspective is more realistic than "everything's great."

When great isn't good enough, positive extremists shift their focus to the greatest. They'll announce, "It's the greatest thing since sliced bread!" What's so hard about slicing bread? Trying not to crush it into a flatbread while you're slicing it is the real challenge. Someone needs to work on the greatest thing since anti-squish sliced bread. Times must have been pretty dull when sliced bread took over as the standard for the category of greatest things since. Bread bakers were delighted after defeating gun manufacturers who were shooting for "it's the greatest thing since silencers." That started the Great Sandwich Boycott of 1928, but to this day sliced bread remains the greatest thing since sliced bread.

The Great Depression was a gloomy time. Optimists spun it as great. Pessimists preferred the Depressing Depression or the Longest, Most Severe Widespread Depression in the History of the World. They did manage to contribute the Stock Market Crash of 1929 and Black Tuesday.

The medical profession soon jumped on the greatness bandwagon. Great doctors originated diagnoses described as great anxiety, great pain, and at great risk. Patients didn't think any of it was great. They put their feet down when physicians attempted to popularize additional positive-sounding symptoms such as merry-go-round vertigo and minty-fresh shortness of breath. It's fuzzy how, but doctors were able to get other charming names approved like maple syrup urine disease (MSUD) and foreign accent syndrome (FAS).

Enough was enough when it came to shakes. Positive and negative doctors debated how to differentiate between great shakes and no great shakes. That's when labeling medical conditions as great slowed. Also banned was telling lactating women to briskly move their bosoms up and down before breastfeeding and treat their children to great milkshakes.

Negative minds countered great anxiety with terms like panic attack, anxiety disorder, throat lumps, and feelings of impending doom. As unsettling as those diagnoses are, positive thinkers still respond to bad medical news with, "Oh, great."

Let's examine a positive and a negative patient experiencing great anxiety. Their symptoms are identical. Both are wearing gowns. Neither knows how to tie it to prevent their ass from being exposed. What are different are their mindsets.

Positive great anxiety patient: "I've been diagnosed with great anxiety. I'm confident my great doctor is on top of it. I'll be feeling great soon."

Negative great anxiety patient (in one breath, without stopping): "I've got an anxiety disorder, and aside from a feeling of tremendous terror, there's tingling in my fingers, toes, and eyelids, plus my throat is closing shut, and I sense I'm suffocating, which is why the room is furiously spinning around like I fell into a centrifuge, causing me to sweat so profusely even my pores are panicking as I drown inside from a typhoon of mind-blowing thoughts overwhelming me—not to mention my heart and the vein on the side of my head are racing at about 178 miles per hour, which is inducing dizziness and provoking near fainting, so I need to lie down before I pass out on your carpet."

The positive patient tricked their mind into believing they'll recover, but they may not, which will be demoralizing. The negative patient knows where they stand. They'll be elated if they recover but grounded in realism should they not.

Negative conditions and disastrous events shouldn't be classified as great. Their effects produce a serious state of mind. Sometimes it's caused by living in a state of chaos. Other times it's the result of living in a state such as Arkansas. Negative thinking is a state of mind too.

Someone may think the great hamburger joint's burgers are great now, yet it'll only take one bad burger to change their mind. Plus after eating all of those greasy hamburgers, how great do you think they will feel years from now when a great cardiologist is stenting them to open a 99-percent-clogged artery? When the doctor breaks the news, they'll also risk feeling great anxiety.

Negativity Scale Checkpoint

Chapter 7: There's Nothing Great about Great

1. **Putting greatness into perspective, I feel like I'm always...**

    a) On a great journey   _____ (5 Points)
    b) Facing great unknowns   _____ (10 Points)
    c) Seen as a great pretender   _____ (15 Points)
    d) Banging my head against the Great Wall   _____ (20 Points)

2. **The negative use of greatness that sounds like me is...**

    a) "It's no great loss."   _____ (5 Points)
    b) "It doesn't sound great."   _____ (10 Points)
    c) "Now's a great time to leave!"   _____ (15 Points)
    d) "What a great mess this is."   _____ (20 Points)

3. **When great anxiety has me hitting the panic button, I'm also ready to...**

    a) Hit the sack   _____ (5 Points)
    b) Hit the brakes   _____ (10 Points)
    c) Hit the roof   _____ (15 Points)
    d) Hit something   _____ (20 Points)

4. **I've spent a great deal of time living in a state of...**

    a) Bliss   _____ (5 Points)
    b) Perpetual déjà vu   _____ (10 Points)
    c) Denial   _____ (15 Points)
    d) Emergency   _____ (20 Points)

5. The great Broadway musical I feel like I'm in when anxiety stages an attack is…

   a) *Pins and Needles*   _____ (5 Points)
   b) *All Shook Up*   _____ (10 Points)
   c) *Jekyll & Hyde*   _____ (15 Points)
   d) *Les Misérables*   _____ (20 Points)

Total Points, Chapter 7   _____

For every positive there's
an even better negative.

-8-

WRECK YOUR DAY THE RIGHT WAY

The consensus on wrecks is they're bad, although body shop owners and tow truck operators aren't complaining. One kind of wreck, however, is a good wreck—a nervous wreck.

Nervous wrecks have a shaky reputation and are unfairly misread. Consider this example based on an almost-true story. Since an elopement wedding was announced twenty-eight hours ago, the bride-to-be's father is a bundle of nerves. In reality he's a savvy, negative-thinking dad worried about his starry-eyed daughter marrying an unemployed, ponytailed pinhead who can't afford a car and skateboards everywhere, whom she met two weeks ago at the annual Mooning of Amtrak event. Dad is directing his nervous energy toward convincing his little girl she could do better with a mail-order groom from Kazakhstan.

Alternatively a positive-thinking dental patient with a rotting tooth isn't nervous before having it pulled. She is unaware the oral surgeon is more jittery than a rodent in a mousetrap factory. His wife is divorcing him and wants the Lexus, the house, and the goldendoodle, but none of the three kids. The optimistic patient is unable to sense any potential problems that might come back to bite her. The overstressed, optimistic oral surgeon risks pulling the wrong tooth, getting sued for malpractice, and blowing his chances of ever dating his hot patient now that he's soon to be single.

Reckoning with being a nervous wreck means learning how to break down your nervousness without causing a breakdown. Once you do you'll be able to handle any case, including a basket case. Contrary to popular and unpopular belief, nervous wrecks aren't accidents waiting to happen. They are accidents waiting to not happen. To clarify this point, let's take a closer look at accidents.

According to the Centers for Disease Control and Prevention, about three million people are nonfatally injured in the US in motor vehicle crashes each year. [3] No matter how positive you are, you could be one of them. Odds multiply by millions more if you drive into your nineties, which happens in places like Florida where licenses are issued to the blind and to geriatrics on walkers who have no feeling in their legs.

Positive thinking won't crashproof you. None of the optimistic drivers who experienced a nonfatal crash hopped out of the car and exclaimed, "I knew it!" Meanwhile no one has bothered to do a study of how many negative thinkers decided not to get into a motor vehicle due to a bad feeling they might get into a wreck. This compelling lack of evidence indirectly implies that negativity may help avoid accidents and possibly save lives.

The solution is to combine being a nervous wreck with being a backseat driver—whether in a car or not. Backseat drivers instinctively sense that whoever is driving has a good chance of getting into an accident. Once your mouth turns into their proverbial wheel, your nervous-wreck consciousness and backseat-driving subconscious merge to infiltrate the driver's terrible-steering consciousness and awful-braking subconscious. Both parties' consciousnesses and subconsciouses simultaneously work together now to avoid a wreck. If all of this sounds confusing, it is, and it isn't.

The reason being a backseat driver also works outside of a car is that there are herds of humans with the capacity to drive you crazy. Nervous wrecks gain an advantage by anticipating everything there is to be shaky, skittish, or spooked about. This doesn't happen in positive à la mode.

Success is dependent on allowing your nervous feelings to flow. Never fight them. This allows your brain, spinal cord, nerves, ganglia, and parts of receptor organs to warn you. Positive thinkers have a lot of nerve when they say, "Calm your nerves." Trying to calm nerves defeats the purpose of what pissed them off in the first place. Your nerves went nuts—and flooded your amygdala with signals, throwing your hypothalamic-pituitary-adrenal axis off by stressing out your emotional and biological stressors—for good reason.

Being a nervous wreck gives your nervous system the freedom to do what it was intended to do, which is protect you from the illusion everything looks fine, but it won't be for long.

The negative advice you acquire throughout this book will point your inner backseat driver in the right direction. Even when you're headed in the wrong direction, you'll know you're going in the right wrong direction.

Negativity Scale Checkpoint

Chapter 8: Wreck Your Day the Right Way

1. A scan of my central nervous system will reveal that my nerves are made of...

    a) Steel _____ (5 Points)
    b) Stone _____ (10 Points)
    c) Stew _____ (15 Points)
    d) String _____ (20 Points)

2. As far as wrecks go, I am a...

    a) Wreck-free spirit _____ (5 Points)
    b) Small wrecking ball _____ (10 Points)
    c) One-person wrecking crew _____ (15 Points)
    d) Train wreck waiting to happen _____ (20 Points)

3. An assessment of my nerve endings will confirm that...

    a) I have attained nervana _____ (5 Points)
    b) I've got a lot of nerve _____ (10 Points)
    c) My nerves are frazzled _____ (15 Points)
    d) I get on everyone's nerves _____ (20 Points)

4. My nerves are the reason I'm involved in more...

    a) Silly accidents _____ (5 Points)
    b) Dumb accidents _____ (10 Points)
    c) Crazy accidents _____ (15 Points)
    d) Hard-to-believe accidents _____ (20 Points)

5. I'm more of a nervous wreck when I'm...

   a) In a pickle   _____ (5 Points)
   b) In the nude   _____ (10 Points)
   c) In the dark   _____ (15 Points)
   d) In a crowd   _____ (20 Points)

   Total Points, Chapter 8   _____

You'll be right more times you
say "I can't" than "I can."

~

-9-

DON'T BELIEVE IT

Do you believe? A better question is: What if you didn't? That's right, entertain the concept of don't believe and you won't believe the results.

Ripley didn't believe everything. Simply by adding "or not" after "believe it," he made an unbelievable fortune by expanding his audience to include skeptics, cynics, agnostics, heretics, and lunatics.

The "believe it" crowd is more accepting. "Or not" folks…not so fast. This is apparent with apparel in terms of applying spray-on clothing. In a blink believers are ready to can their entire wardrobe. Nonbelievers need a barrage of questions answered first such as:

"Where do I keep my keys?"

"What happens if it rains?" and

"Do spray-on zippers hurt when they get stuck?"

It doesn't mean negative-thinking nonbelievers are not open minded or less clothes minded. What it does indicate is that when you believe someone is the kind of person who will give you the shirt off their back, you can also believe it's going to be much harder for them to do it if it's sprayed on.

Jillions of hopefuls are peering out windows right now, believing Publishers Clearing House is on the way to deliver their first weekly check for life. They have a better chance of seeing a neighbor's home get burglarized than they do of receiving a penny from this sweepstakes. Zillions of females who were in good health yesterday—and believed they would be today—learned they have an infection. It gets extra frustrating for women who will be uninvited to seders during Passover if it's a yeast infection. Conglomerations of singles believe they are going to meet someone on a dating app who looks like their photos. As if that's going to happen without a time machine.

These scenarios all have one thing in common: the chances of what the players involved hope will come true are low. When someone believes they can do something or envisions something will happen the way they expect, it doesn't mean they can or it will.

What have you got to lose by joining the can't-believe camp? This unsanctioned plan exposes how.

Three-Step Disbeliever Detox

Step 1: Organize Your Disbelief System

You know the feeling when you can't believe your eyes or ears? All four of them are trying to tell you something. Let the feeling spread to your liver, kidneys, lungs, colon, and other organs. Train them to instant message your brain when they're not in a believing mood too.

Message from your lungs: "The garbage coming out of that person's mouth inflames my alveoli."

Message from your colon: "Something stinks here, and it isn't me."

Step 2: Push Back with Resistance Training

Voluntary and involuntary muscles contract when you don't believe. Strengthen them with:

> Rebuff Repetitions: Flex your cold shoulders.
> Rejection Therapy: When you feel the burn—spurn.
> Opposition Endurance: Don't deny you're in denial.

> Contradiction Toning: Relieve pain; go against the grain.
> Increase Wait Limits: Dumbbells are quick to believe.

Step 3: Flush Out Belief Waste Matter

When believing fails you, poisonous toxins build up. Do a nonbeliever mental cleanse to wash them away. Let your negative thoughts flow and soothe you as you repeatedly repeat them, redundantly, over and over, time and again…

> "I am not gullible and take no gullibull."
> "It is not a sin to be a cynic."
> "My skeptic tank is full."
> "I'm the dissenter of the universe."
> "Kiss my rebuttal."

Nonbelieving requires mind-bending and tongue-twisting practice. When someone shares news, reply with, "I don't believe it!" They'll think what they revealed was so incredible, it was too unbelievable for you to believe. That's how Ripley got started. Believe it…or not.

Negativity Scale Checkpoint

Chapter 9: Don't Believe It

1. **I have the hardest time believing...**

   a) It's not butter   _____ (5 Points)
   b) It's not you, it's me   _____ (10 Points)
   c) It's not my fault   _____ (15 Points)
   d) It's not going to stop   _____ (20 Points)

2. **My philosophy when it comes to believing is to trust everyone as if they are a...**

   a) Saint   _____ (5 Points)
   b) Savant   _____ (10 Points)
   c) Senator   _____ (15 Points)
   d) Snake oil salesman   _____ (20 Points)

3. **Believe it or not, one thing I enjoy giving people is...**

   a) Lots of encouragement   _____ (5 Points)
   b) An earful of advice   _____ (10 Points)
   c) A look like I'm unhinged   _____ (15 Points)
   d) The finger   _____ (20 Points)

4. **More things happen to me that...**

   a) Ripley wouldn't believe   _____ (5 Points)
   b) I'd prefer not to believe   _____ (10 Points)
   c) In a million years, you'd never believe   _____ (15 Points)
   d) Are make believe   _____ (20 Points)

5. When someone tells me something I find hard to swallow, I will…

   a) Chew on it slowly   _____ (5 Points)
   b) Bite down, grin, and bear it _____ (10 Points)
   c) Spit out something crazy back _____ (15 Points)
   d) Choke on it   _____ (20 Points)

Total Points, Chapter 9   _____

If you put your mind to it,
everything is impossible.

~

-10-

GET INTO DOUBT

You may think doubt is bad. Many authorities on ambiguity question that viewpoint. The uncertainty surrounding doubt is created by not making decisions with conviction. In this case conviction has nothing to do with your arrest record, if you have one—although it is a crime to let doubt make you feel like you're a prisoner of it.

When you learn to doubt without apprehension, you're empowered to explore alternative options you'd never have considered. Take the story of Thomas...

The apostle Thomas was a disciple of Jesus. He didn't believe Jesus arose from the dead. In his defense it wasn't like resurrection was trendy yet, so he had good reason to be skeptical. An assemblage of adherents told Thomas they saw the Lord in person. Gossipers later confirmed this occurred at the popular Zealots & Evangelists Tavern downtown. Thomas demanded proof, but no photos existed. It was around AD 33, and cameras hadn't been invented. Thomas attended the next disciple gathering, saw Jesus for himself, and satisfied his doubt. The moral of the story is: it's better to doubt than to be double-crossed by your friends. Even Jesus would agree.

You don't have to be named Thomas to doubt. If you hear of a resurrection for someone you know, doubt it until you see proof. Why accept anyone's word before you verify it? After another beer or two, who knows what those disciples might boast about? Next thing you know, they could also claim they resurrected Julius Caesar, Hippocrates, and Confucius.

Other books encourage you to focus on overcoming doubt. Why bother? It doesn't require a PhD in doubtology to decipher why doubt is nothing more than dubious doubletalk. "I doubt this" means you don't approve. "I don't doubt that" translates to you agree. When you go beyond a doubt, how far do you go, and why does it only work with reasonable doubts? Ask an architect how much room to leave for doubt. They have no clue. Of all the doubts you've ever had, have you ever seen one with a shadow? Go to a nursery and ask what brand they recommend for planting seeds of doubt. Without an answer it's impossible to understand how doubts grow. One thing is clear: be skeptical of doubts.

"I have no doubts" is another nonsensical comment. Why mention doubts if you don't have any? Would you go on a job interview and blurt out, "I have no ambition"? Or disclose to a giraffe at the zoo, "I have no neck"? Volunteering information about what you don't have is how doubt creeps into conversations and penetrates your psyche. This is different than having laryngitis and mouthing, "I have no words," which would not be in doubt.

Another tip is never give yourself the benefit of the doubt. Benefits are positive. Doubt is negative. The two don't mix. Look for the drawback of the doubt instead. Once you weigh the drawbacks, you can deal with them. Positive thinkers only see the benefit of the doubt. Without seeing the drawback of the doubt, it's impossible to reap the full benefits. This paragraph clearly captures why doubts are difficult to express.

No doubt you've lost count of all the times you were told, "Don't doubt yourself." If you do have an accurate calculation, it's time to explore new hobbies. Not doubting yourself can be disastrous advice. It inspires a sense of security that allows you to move forward in situations where you should retreat. You're then left vulnerable to getting your butt kicked, whereas you might have had good reason to doubt yourself in the first place.

When you don't see the negative side of doubts, a gnawing feeling of uncertainty eats away at you like moths in a closet full of moist fabrics. This is relevant since moths have an affinity for wool sweaters, while having no doubts allows you to let someone pull the wool over your eyes. It's too bad moths aren't attracted to doubts the way they are to floodlights. Doubts would be easier to see and you'd be able to spot the holes in them. You can try a reenactment of this mesmerizing visual by writing down your doubts, shining a bright flashlight on them, and shooting holes through each one on your own. Wearing a wool sweater is optional.

Doubt everything. Doubt nothing. Doubt yourself. It's impossible to remove all doubt, especially when a myriad of situations and circumstances are in doubt or beyond doubt. From now on, exercise doubt clout. Make a conscious effort to doubt your doubts. It's the only way to rid yourself of them.

Negativity Scale Checkpoint

Chapter 10: Get into Doubt

1. **A scan of my head taken this second would reveal...**

    a) There's not a doubt in my mind   _____ (5 Points)
    b) Little is in doubt   _____ (10 Points)
    c) I'm full of doubt   _____ (15 Points)
    d) You should doubt everything about
       me, even my answer to this question   _____ (20 Points)

2. **After reading this chapter, I doubt I will ...**

    a) Doubt more   _____ (5 Points)
    b) Not doubt the same   _____ (10 Points)
    c) Doubt less   _____ (15 Points)
    d) Ever doubt my doubts   _____ (20 Points)

3. **Of all the ways to doubt, I'm most skilled at...**

    a) Sensing doubt   _____ (5 Points)
    b) Removing doubt   _____ (10 Points)
    c) Casting doubt   _____ (15 Points)
    d) Feeling doubt beyond
       a shadow of it   _____ (20 Points)

4. **The level of doubt I carry around during a typical week is...**

    a) Near my ankles   _____ (5 Points)
    b) Hovering around my waist   _____ (10 Points)
    c) Chest high   _____ (15 Points)
    d) Way over my head   _____ (20 Points)

5. The room that leaves most room for doubt is my...

   a) Bathroom   _____ (5 Points)
   b) Living room   _____ (10 Points)
   c) Dining room   _____ (15 Points)
   d) Bedroom   _____ (20 Points)

Total Points, Chapter 10   _____

The good thing about misery is it loves company, so you're never alone.

-11-

XXXXXXXXXXXXXXXXX

Chapter eleven has been filed, and upon reorganization, converted into chapter seven and chapter thirteen.

Positive people have more problems with bankruptcy by perceiving debt as something outstanding.

-12-

BLAME YOURSELF

At a young age, we learn to blame others. Anyone who has brothers or sisters knows this well. Thora, a preteen, wants to get her brother, Sven, in trouble. She buys a can of red spray paint and writes in extremely large letters on the garage wall, "Thora is a bitch!" No way her parents will blame her for writing that about herself. Sven gets grounded for two weeks and has to paint the garage.

Sven craves payback. He's aware Thora is starting to curse and writes all over his mom's perfume bottles, "Phuk," and "Schit." At the family hearing, Sven pleads, "I know how to spell ef-u-cee-kay and ess-aitch-i-tee!" This time the parents, Erika and Erik Erikson, blame Thora for the boxfitti and hold Sven in contempt for using foul language.

The war between Thora and Sven rages for three more nonstop, he-did-it, she-did-it years. Erika and Erik finally waive the Swiss flag and enroll them at Our Lady of Perpetually Troubled Girls and Antagonistic Boys School in Oslo. Erik messes up and discovers too late the school is in Oslo, Minnesota, not Oslo, Norway. He blames Google.

Erika and Erik continue to argue and blame each other. Erika spray paints on the garage wall, "Erik is a bastard!" For those of you who don't speak Swedish, "bastard" means bastard. Erika blames Erik for working all the time, never being around to help her, and not making time for the kids. Erik blames the economy. They divorce months later.

Erika moves in with her parents, Freya and Fridolf. She blames them for not preparing her for motherhood or marriage. Freya denies all charges, and Fridolf calls the school in Oslo to inquire whether they take adult children. They do not, but a school in Oslo, Florida, does accept older folks. This case study is a classic example of how there's enough blame to go around the world for everyone.

By the time we become grown-ups, our blaming skills are honed at work, in relationships, and for interactions involving animate or inanimate objects. It's fascinating when someone who isn't paying attention walks into a streetlight pole and growls, "Stupid pole!" Yes, it was the pole's fault. Everyone knew how dangerous poles were the moment they mastered telekinesis.

This backward logic is illogical. Anyone can point fingers, but even the middle finger is pointed upward, not directly at the target. The only one who should be blamed for anything is yourself. Taking the hit personally is easier—and less complicated—than blaming someone else.

When you blame others, chances are they'll deny it. This is the beauty of blaming yourself. After resigning yourself to taking the blame, you'll develop impenetrable, thick skin, and people will love you more. Not because your skin is thicker or lovelier, but how could they not appreciate you after you've said, "It's my fault," especially if they did it?

At first you may feel guilty about pleading guilty when you know you're not guilty. Worry not. After a while people will get sick of you taking the blame and respond with:

"It's no big deal,"

"Don't be so hard on yourself," and

"You're being silly; my bad."

Think of it as reverse psychology in reverse. Blame causes the recipient to go on the defensive and feel hurt. If you always take the blame, the other party becomes suspicious and questions why you're the one at fault every time. They'll debate themselves to probe whether they were more at fault than initially thought. Once you announce, "It's my fault," the conversation changes to:

"No, no, it's my fault!"

"Wrong! I'm at fault!"

"No, please fault me!"

In the blame game, there are three rules to the exception:

Rule 1: Don't take the blame if your sex life will suffer.
Rule 2: If it costs you money, you didn't do it.
Rule 3: Never take responsibility for a fart. Blame a dog, cat, old lady, chair cushion, fly—anyone or anything other than you.

Blaming has evolved into a complex skill. There's no one to even blame for that. Deciding whether to place, put, lay, or assign blame is a hair-pulling process, yet not everyone who does it appears to have patches of yanked-out hair.

Once you accept taking the blame, whenever anyone else blames you it won't bother you since you wanted to be blamed. Blame is designed to be shifted. After you make it stationary, you'll have no one to blame but yourself.

Negativity Scale Checkpoint

Chapter 12: Blame Yourself

1. **When I play the blame game, my strategy is...**

    a) Follow the rules   _____ (5 Points)
    b) Stretch the rules   _____ (10 Points)
    c) Play by my own rules   _____ (15 Points)
    d) Wait, there are rules?   _____ (20 Points)

2. **One ability I have that could someday land me in the Hall of Blame is I'm a...**

    a) Fantastic finger pointer   _____ (5 Points)
    b) Phenomenal fault finder   _____ (10 Points)
    c) World-class accuser rebuker   _____ (15 Points)
    d) Badass bad mouther   _____ (20 Points)

3. **I blame more situations for going haywire in my life on my...**

    a) Lousy luck   _____ (5 Points)
    b) Laziness   _____ (10 Points)
    c) Loud mouth   _____ (15 Points
    d) Loony parents   _____ (20 Points)

4. **In sports, the blame for losing should be put on...**

    a) Awful referees   _____ (5 Points)
    b) Rude fans   _____ (10 Points)
    c) Strip clubs   _____ (15 Points)
    d) Games being fixed   _____ (20 Points)

5. **Putting ego aside, I'll usually take the blame…**

   a) When it's my fault or to keep the peace   _____ (5 Points)
   b) Because my Bible says so   _____ (10 Points)
   c) Never—I'll deny ever being there
       if I have to   _____ (15 Points)
   d) Always—most of the time I did it   _____ (20 Points)

Total Points, Chapter 12   _____

There is no point in standing for what you believe when you can do it sitting down.

~

-13-

NO LUCK IS THE BEST LUCK

Good luck and bad luck no longer cover it all. After pioneering luck seekers concluded that they could create their own luck, the gates of good fortune burst open. Novices jumped to trademark beginner's luck. The sight challenged had their own vision for blind luck. Proponents of virginity rushed to claim pure luck. Morons made a play for dumb luck. Artists answered back with a campaign focused on the luck of the draw. Even men suffering from erectile dysfunction got into the act, grasping for a stroke of luck. With all of these different kinds of luck taken, losers were left shit out of luck.

We're at the mercy of luck. When it runs out, we're reminded how merely mortal we are. The luckiest lucky charms can't keep anyone's positive streak going indefinitely. Owning a rabbit's foot—or feet if you purchase them in pairs for double luck—isn't a cure for unluckiness. Besides, how lucky is the rabbit? Millions of little rabbit tootsies are sold each year. It's mind boggling we don't see rabbits everywhere on crutches, in little wheelchairs, or zipping around on teensy Segways. They can't even move when someone dangles a carrot in front of them. Turtles mock them for being slow.

Carrying around a horseshoe won't turn you into a lucky winner either. Plenty of racehorses running around wearing four of these hyped lucky shoes still get trounced race after race. As do the bettors putting money on them. According to an unpublished and unofficial gallop poll, results imply that an unknown percentage of jockeys vote neigh on whether horseshoes get them any closer to the winner's circle of life.

Let's not forget four-leaf clovers, which are widely believed to symbolize faith, hope, love, and luck. Your odds of finding one are one in ten thousand. [4] Why stop there? Clovers with many more leaves exist. According to Guinness World Records, the most leaves on a clover are fifty-six. [5] Yet you never hear of anyone promoting how it can bring you fourteen times the luck of a four-leaf clover. Luckaticians believe the failure to make this connection is linked to having no luck with math.

The number thirteen is considered unlucky. A majority of buildings with elevators don't have a thirteenth button or a thirteenth floor. Unlucky elevator riders still get stuck or break down on other-numbered floors, making every destination a potential bad luck stop. If this continues, the numberers behind getting button thirteen and floor thirteen banned might not stop there. One day buildings may only contain stairways and elevators, with no floors.

Note: This book does have a chapter thirteen. Unlike elevator riders, triskaidekaphobia doesn't affect people who can read.

Optimists believe they have good luck. Yet it's impossible for them to positive think their way to overcoming what's out of their control. If they go without bathing for two weeks, they'd be lucky not to contract dermatitis neglecta. Washing is especially important to remember anytime you have skin in the game. It's horrible luck if a brick falls off a building and hits an optimist on the head. No matter how lucky they feel, the impact of a brain-jolting brick on the noggin is not lessened, which in itself is a lessened to be learned.

As luck would have it, you can't rely on luck. Everyone is lucky or unlucky sooner or later. A slot player will hit a big jackpot at a casino. A bar patron somewhere is going to get hit in the face by a flying fist. A select group of professional hockey players are destined to take home the Stanley Cup. Many more are doomed to get hit in the cup and go home clutching their crotches.

Luck doesn't guarantee future results either. It can't ensure that the jackpot winner won't go broke. The bar patron's face might not look as handsome after healing. There's no assurance that a player will win the

Stanley Cup again or that a one-hundred-mile-per-hour slapshot won't bust his balls another time.

When positive thinkers believe in luck, they're the ones who get zapped the hardest once it changes. With no luck and negative thinking, you won't hope to win a fortune, but you'll be much better prepared for misfortune. You may not close a big deal, and when you don't, you'll be able to easily accept it's no big deal. You can still get a promotion or a raise, but you may have to outwork luckier people. If that doesn't work, there's always the old-fashioned way—sleep with an influential decision maker, which is another effective way to get lucky.

With or without luck, whatever is going to happen is going to happen. This is why having the consistency of no luck is the best luck of all.

Negativity Scale Checkpoint

Chapter 13: No Luck Is the Best Luck

1. **The best way to describe the luck I've been blessed with is...**

    a) Leprechauns are jealous   _____ (5 Points)
    b) Black cats run from me   _____ (10 Points)
    c) Casinos cheer when I walk in   _____ (15 Points)
    d) Pigeons crap on my head a lot   _____ (20 Points)

2. **One thing that would improve my luck is...**

    a) A lucky break   _____ (5 Points)
    b) A lucky dog   _____ (10 Points)
    c) Man, trans, or lady luck   _____ (15 Points)
    d) The luck of the devil   _____ (20 Points)

3. **As for my parents' luck, after one year with me they were probably thinking...**

    a) "We've got a winner!"   _____ (5 Points)
    b) "It could have been worse."   _____ (10 Points)
    c) "Glad we didn't have twins."   _____ (15 Points)
    d) "If we divorce, you can have full custody."   _____ (20 Points)

4. **You can bet whatever I bet on will usually result in someone saying or thinking...**

    a) "You know how to pick 'em."   _____ (5 Points)
    b) "You lucky dog!"   _____ (10 Points)
    c) "What were you thinking?"   _____ (15 Points)
    d) "How hard did you hit your head?"   _____ (20 Points)

5. The luck I've had this past year...

   a) Has double rainbows forming
      over me   _____ (5 Points)
   b) Was determined by eeny,
      meeny, miny, and moe   _____ (10 Points)
   c) Explains why the stalls I go into
      in public restrooms never have
      toilet paper   _____ (15 Points)
   d) Incites owls to hoot at me   _____ (20 Points)

Total Points, Chapter 13   _____

When things go to hell, would
you want to be an optimist?

∽

-14-

DON'T PUT OFF PROCRASTINATION

Once Merriam and Webster finally got around to defining procrastination, they came up with "to put off intentionally the doing of something that should be done." In the world of negativity, we're all for putting off the doing of what should be done. We know we're doing it on purpose too. That's why we're not doing it. For good reason since the sooner we do it, the quicker we might regret doing it. By not doing it, we're avoiding the consequences of what doing it could do to us. All of this could lead to our undoing, which wouldn't do anyone any good.

Too bad Hamlet was such a self-centered ham. If he were a procrastinator, "to be or not to be" might have been "to do or not to do." Maybe then he wouldn't have been responsible for the deaths of Polonius, Laertes, Claudius, Rosencrantz, and Guildenstern, effectively ending any chance of them joining forces to create a formidable law firm.

Positive thinkers believe procrastination is a waiting game to avoid playing. They'll prod, "Stop procrastinating and make a decision already," or caution, "You're going to drive yourself crazy if you keep procrastinating." It's the same kind of rah-rah rationale behind Benjamin Franklin's, "Don't put off until tomorrow what you can do today." Meanwhile Ben was out flying a kite with a key attached under thunderclouds, trying to prove lightning was electrical in nature. This type of thinking, without permanent procrastination, could have resulted in nonscientific minds discovering that the key to this experiment may include them doing an impersonation of an insect flying into a bug zapper.

Scarlett O'Hara of *Gone with the Wind* fame frankly didn't give a damn about the consequence of procrastination. When she needed more time to think, her reply was, "After all, tomorrow is another day." In Scarlett's day, back in the 1860s, no one had calendar apps or sticky notes. Consequently dilly dalliers with poor note-taking skills and dawdlers possessing bad memories were deemed idlers and lingerers by default. They never remembered what they had to do, so it never got done. If you've been putting off things your entire life with this approach, you've got the right idea. Congratulations on all the money you've saved on day planners.

While positive thinkers instinctively gravitate toward "I can do it," negative thinkers do well with "Ah, why bother." Delays can transition into satisfying rest periods. Lags often turn into delightful drags. Stringing people along elicits feelings of joy few ever experience other than marionettists.

Procrastination puts you in charge of the unnecessary. Nothing happens until you say so. Everyone is at your mercy until further notice. There's no question you're going to be bugged—not necessarily by spies working for foreign governments, although that's possible—but by others who want you to do what they want, when they want. Think of procrastination as your bug repellent. Use it to extinguish unwanted requests or demands from pests.

Extreme procrastinators have been known to go too far. The trick to proficient, prolonged hesitancy is knowing what to delay and for how long. An obscure urological proverb puts this into perspective: "Putting off peeing pains your bladder, then urine trouble." A modern-day translation from Brooklyn is, "Piss off! I'll get to it when I get to it."

Focus on what doesn't matter, which is what a majority of your day consists of anyway. Put off everything you don't have to do today. Procrastinate about what would happen if you never got to it. When you procrastinate about cleaning your home, how long can you hold out—until you see dust everywhere, or until roaches are eating all the dog's food before the dog? Are there calls you've held off on returning for days, weeks, or months? Will they call you back or never talk to you again, and if you never hear from them again, is it a bad thing? Is the creaky step going upstairs as dangerous as it's going to get, or could you fall in and join the creepy horror movie creatures who live under the stairs?

Forget trying to be a decision maker. Feel what it's like as a non-decision-maker. Caboodles of decision makers are decisioning all day long and getting nothing done. By procrastinating and making fewer or no decisions, at the least you'll be reducing the number of awful decisions you make.

Set some time to procrastinate about procrastinating. Take your time; there's no rush.

Negativity Scale Checkpoint

Chapter 14: Don't Put off Procrastination

1. **If a psychotherapist of procrastination analyzed me, they would conclude...**

    a) I dread delaying anything   _____ (5 Points)
    b) I'm a fan of later, sometimes   _____ (10 Points)
    c) I am lazy, lazy, lazy   _____ (15 Points)
    d) I'll get back to you on that   _____ (20 Points)

2. **One part of procrastination I love is...**

    a) More time to think   _____ (5 Points)
    b) It makes my calendar look full   _____ (10 Points)
    c) Breaking my last delay record   _____ (15 Points)
    d) How much it annoys people   _____ (20 Points)

3. **I would do a lot more procrastinating if it didn't...**

    a) Make me feel guilty   _____ (5 Points)
    b) Take so long   _____ (10 Points)
    c) Interfere with all the other stuff I've put on hold   _____ (15 Points)
    d) Lead to more people yelling at or threatening me   _____ (20 Points)

4. **When I'm committed to initiating a delay, the longest I can hold off for is....**

    a) Five to ten minutes   _____ (5 Points)
    b) Twenty-four hours, but not on the same day   _____ (10 Points)
    c) Until I'm in the mood   _____ (15 Points)
    d) When noses stop running   _____ (20 Points)

5. **A revised version of the proverb that best positions my procrastination strategy is...**

   a) Bite off more than you can chew   _____ (5 Points)
   b) Good things come to those who
      don't wait   _____ (10 Points)
   c) Strike while the iron is cold   _____ (15 Points)
   d) Better never than late   _____ (20 Points)

Total Points, Chapter 14   _____

If positive-thinking people are so positive,
why are they so against negative thinking?

-15-

IT'S CRITICAL TO BE CRITICAL

Professor Quincy Adams Wagstaff, president of Huxley College, put it best when he declared, "Whatever it is, I'm against it." [6] If you're not against whatever it is, when it doesn't work out it works against you. Analyzing situations in plain sight requires negative foresight. Otherwise the chances of regret in positive hindsight lead to discontent. Now that that's clear, you'll need to develop critical skills for anticipating all the reasons to be against whatever it is.

Unsupported studies prove beyond an unreasonable doubt how tough it is to take someone at face value. Next time you look a person in the face, calculate how much value you see. Is it a face that belongs on a coffee mug or a wanted poster? Would you classify them as a bald-faced liar, even if they have a beard? How about a woman with a thick moustache? What's written all over her face? Are there typos and grammatical errors? Do they have a blank look, or are the blanks filled in with Botox? Can you tell if there's egg on their face? Is the rest of their meal on their shirt, blouse, or lap? Are there signs they're spiteful—like redness around the nostrils where they might have tried to cut off their nose? Is it the kind of face only a mother with two detached retinas could love?

There are many wrinkles to consider when evaluating humans or people who can't possibly be human at face value. It's even harder to appraise when dealing with anyone who's two faced or had a facelift, whereby the original face value has been stretched or inflated, sometimes too far.

The devaluation of face value has made criticism an invaluable necessity for your negativity toolbox. Unlike passing gas or a kidney stone, passing judgment has a longer-term effect. Here's what to keep in mind:

Top Six Components of Critical Thinking

Component 1: Few at Work Know Squat
If you owned the company where you work, how many current employee salaries would chew away at you like teeth at a rib-eating competition? What's the number of asses you'd need to light a fire under with a blowtorch? Are there more staff members you'd like to take out to lunch or who are mentally out to lunch? Be critical of coworkers. They're often wrong or boneheads. Whatever they say or do, resist it.

Component 2: What You Buy Will Fail
Products are designed to quit working at the most inconvenient times. Your air conditioning unit is going to fail on a Friday night in the middle of the hottest summer in twenty years. Shiny new tires will wear out or blow in the pouring rain as you're rushing somewhere important. Stay ahead of the inevitable and don't always buy what companies say about their products.

Component 3: Ideas Suck
Bad ideas spread faster than a gymnast's legs doing a jump split. Ideas are cheap too. For the longest time, they've sold for less than roses, bagels, and donuts at a dime a dozen. An idea isn't good unless it will make you rich, richer, or less unhappy. If an idea falls apart, which most do, let it be your own. Otherwise press the reject button.

Component 4: Put Everything under a Microscope
Everyone is hiding front-page tabloid news. Could you do business with a person who claims they were once abducted in Colorado and fondled by gender-neutral aliens from outer space? Are you cool hanging out with someone who enjoys demonstrating how their breath wilts plants? Would you think differently of a guest at a party who is incapable of

laughing and meows instead? Be critical of people before you uncover what could make them flee to Argentina and go into hiding.

Component 5: Take Feelings into Consideration
Morris Albert repeated the word "feelings" twenty-three times [7] in a three-minute-and-forty-six-second song called "Feelings," which is a record. The secret to delivering what's on your critical mind is dispersing it with feelings, nothing more than feelings. Focus on the feelings that make you say, "Wo-o-o."

Component 6: Criticize Based on Brain Size
Dish out criticism in proportion to the size of the recipient's brain. The average brain weighs about three pounds. Therefore the amount of criticism you offer should vary between pea-sized brains, masterminds, and everything in between.

You don't have to be a critically acclaimed critic to criticize or critique. All you have to remember is these three critical words: "I'm against it."

Negativity Scale Checkpoint

Chapter 15: It's Critical to Be Critical

1. When an approval is required, my nature is to vote…

   a) "For it." _____ (5 Points)
   b) "I'll think about it." _____ (10 Points)
   c) "No way," if I'm sober. _____ (15 Points)
   d) "I'll let you know when hamsters sing." _____ (20 Points)

2. The main thing I could highlight on a critical thinking résumé is my…

   a) Well-developed critical eye _____ (5 Points)
   b) Dead-on critical feedback _____ (10 Points)
   c) Ability to commit critical errors _____ (15 Points)
   d) List of critical needs _____ (20 Points)

3. I'm more critical of people who are…

   a) Living under a rock _____ (5 Points)
   b) Living on the edge _____ (10 Points)
   c) Living in a van _____ (15 Points)
   d) Living anywhere _____ (20 Points)

4. If a critic critiqued my style of criticizing, they would categorize it as…

   a) Nonexistent _____ (5 Points)
   b) Nonthreatening _____ (10 Points)
   c) Nonspecific _____ (15 Points)
   d) Nonsensical _____ (20 Points)

5. When I analyze and scrutinize, I'm relying on...

    a) Nearsighted insight   _____ (5 Points)
    b) Farsighted foresight   _____ (10 Points)
    c) Shortsighted hindsight   _____ (15 Points)
    d) Unsighted oversight   _____ (20 Points)

Total Points, Chapter 15   _____

Even beds have a wrong side to get up on.

-16-

PLAYING DUMB ISN'T BEING STUPID

There is an intelligence shortage rapidly spreading everywhere people and buffalo roam. Unsubstantiated white papers report that the odds of encountering multiple ignoramuses every day you're inhaling and exhaling is a harsh reality.

Positive thinkers are more accepting of the growing not-so-smart segment of society. It's their nature to encourage, motivate, and offer hope. Yet no matter how much effort they put into supporting those whose brain lights function on a dimmer, no one put it better than Forrest Gump, who brilliantly said, "Stupid is as stupid does."

Negative thinkers are instinctively programmed to be less tolerant of twits, nitwits, half-wits, and dimwits as well as numskulls, nincompoops, and knuckleheads. Pessimists analyze everything negatively, which is necessary to pinpointing all potential worst-case scenarios. Constant communication exchanges with the brain are required to absorb a relentless flow of annoyances, aggravations, and agonies. This arguably provides disputable, somewhat-clear evidence indicating negative-driven intelligence can be harnessed to achieve happiness in an increasingly dumb and dumber world.

Creating a distinct advantage among the enormous brainpower-deficient population is a shrewd opportunity for negative thinkers. It is important to remember that whatever optimists say to those whose brainwaves barely register on an electroencephalography test goes in one ear and out the other. When you expose them to your negative side, they'll become even more confused. Negative brain vibe transference overloading (NBVTO) goes even further in its capacity to mess with the limited brain capacity of others.

While interacting with those who are short on smarts, you can use your smarts to play dumb, and they'll never catch on. It's a foolproof strategy since fools are unable to fool anyone other than themselves. Don't underestimate the power of pretending to be dumb. Unintelligent people are born that way or did something along the way to fry massive quantities of brain cells. Smart people have to work at being unintelligent. There is a fine line between blending in with the brainless and being confused as one of them.

Let positive thinkers burn time showing unintelligent people the bright side. Here is how you can learn to test intellectual limitations during conversations with airheads across a variety of real-life and brain-on-pause scenarios…

Five Astute Play-Dumb Self Put Downs

You can get away with more by revealing less brain.

> "Have you read my mother's book, *I Prayed for a Doctor but Got a Dummkopf*?"
> "Now you can see why I didn't get into Stanford."
> "Every day feels like April Fools' Day to me."
> "Please take me to the stupid police station so I can turn myself in."
> "I was the only kid at school who got stung by a spelling bee."

Five Clever Play-Dumb Compliments

One way to play down your intelligence is to make whomever you're with feel smarter than you.

> "You should try out for *Jeopardy!*"
> "How do you know so much? Did you memorize Wikipedia?"
> "Why aren't you solving crimes for the FBI?"
> "How long does it take you to do a Rubik's cube—eight seconds?"
> "Are recruiters from Mensa calling you all week?"

Five Brainy Play-Dumb Chat Initiators

Fun things happen when oral exchanges get off on a foolish foot.

> "Is it me, or have you also been meeting a lot of stupid people lately?"
> "A mannequin is smarter than your manager. Why aren't you running this place?" *(wink)*
> "Do you know any dumb people jokes? They make me feel smarter."
> "What am I trying to say? Feel free to put words in my mouth."
> "Is Taco Tuesday always on Tuesday?"

It's been said there's no such thing as a stupid question. Of course someone stupid was the first one to say that. As we're growing up, parents don't help with questions like, "How stupid are you?"

"Well, I do have your genes, Mom."

One thing you should always question, however, is the intelligence of others. Once you have the answer, you'll know who's being stupid, and who's playing dumb.

Negativity Scale Checkpoint

Chapter 16: Playing Dumb Isn't Being Stupid

1. **Playing dumb is something…**

    a) I'm clueless at   _____ (5 Points)
    b) I'm getting smarter at   _____ (10 Points)
    c) I'm a natural at   _____ (15 Points)
    d) I'm so good at, people do think I'm dumb   _____ (20 Points)

2. **I'd be more likely to say…**

    a) "I'm not stupid."   _____ (5 Points)
    b) "That's stupid."   _____ (10 Points)
    c) "You're stupid!"   _____ (15 Points)
    d) "Is everyone here stupid?"   _____ (20 Points)

3. **I tend to treat people who lack intelligence like…**

    a) They're smarter than they are   _____ (5 Points)
    b) There's someplace else I have to be   _____ (10 Points)
    c) A source of entertainment   _____ (15 Points)
    d) I'm Einstein and they're a doorknob   _____ (20 Points)

4. **If the IRS did a stupid audit on me, I'd have more deductions to claim on…**

    a) Stupid excuses   _____ (5 Points)
    b) Stupid mistakes   _____ (10 Points)
    c) Stupid arguments   _____ (15 Points)
    d) Stupid obsessions   _____ (20 Points)

5. **When my brain fills with negative thoughts, it is more likely I will...**

   a) Cover my ears   _____ (5 Points)
   b) Cover my eyes   _____ (10 Points)
   c) Cover my tracks   _____ (15 Points)
   d) Cover my ass   _____ (20 Points)

   Total Points, Chapter 16   _____

Why worry about tomorrow when there
is so much to worry about today?

-17-

SUCCEED AT FAILURE

From the time we can talk, optimists teach us to seek success. No wonder we have a slew of four-year-olds who tell anyone visiting their home, "I'm going to Harvard!" The bulk of them can't even pronounce it. They're heading to Harwood, or in Boston, Havid. The truth is no parent wants to hear their precious little offspring announce to company, "I'm going to Wonkadonka Community College!"

It's all a sham, anyway. Only a mere handful of kids in the world who declare they're going to Harvard or any other prestigious school ever go. Little-known studies swept under the rug by elite universities imply that from the entire universe of potential students, the vast majority have a significantly higher chance of catching poison ivy than they do of scratching their way into an Ivy League institution. The smartest plan is to attend any school that accepts you and visit Harvard. You won't be lying now when you tell people you went to Harvard.

Regardless of education, it's impossible to succeed without failing first. Why not shoot for failure right from the get-go? Thomas Edison understood this approach. Edison withstood a great deal of heckling from friends, family, colleagues, and strangers when he failed repeatedly at trying to figure out where he went wrong. The way he saw it was, "I have not failed ten thousand times—I've successfully found ten thousand ways that will not work." [8] Imagine using this defense with a teacher or professor after failing dozens of tests, including the midterm and final exams. They would not appreciate this kind of backsliding and advise you to find another career path.

It is unclear whether Edison was an exaggerator, but it is dark as night he was adept at flopping on the way to success. To make his accomplishments even more impressive, before Edison invented the light bulb he had no choice but to work by candlelight and then torch. Maybe that's why he kept failing. With the window open on windy days, it would be lights out. When there was an animal fat shortage to power the burning of candles and torches, notes scribbled by townspeople purportedly describe how he rubbed two sticks together and came close to burning down the house on dozens of occasions.

If you feel like you've been struggling, you may only be nine or ten thousand attempts short of hitting on something big. Coincidentally this entire book was rewritten more than ten thousand times, and countless light bulbs blew out in the process.

One misconception about success is it can happen overnight. It rarely does unless it involves a spectacular one-night stand. An unclassified study of overnight successes indicates that people will tell you they are an overnight success but leave out the part it was a long night, which lasted years to decades. Don't get fooled when positive thinkers tell you the night is young. It still won't increase your chances of becoming an overnight success by thinking the night still has time to get older. Neither will the extra hour you bank one night in the fall, courtesy of daylight saving time.

Forward-thinking pessimists believe success is elusive and failure is probable. They were the ones who spread the word that success isn't guaranteed. Nevertheless tens of hundreds of thousands of millions of optimists continue to sell the "You can become a success too" story. To complicate things, many costs are now associated with success. Even if you have success, there is a price to pay for it. This is why optimists introduced money-back guarantees. Savvy pessimists know what money-back guarantees are—failure insurance policies.

Positive thinkers acknowledge that success isn't enough to stand on its own, which is why they launched "Success begets success." This confused a lot of people who don't have a clue what a long, narrow loaf of French bread sandwiched between two successes has to do with anything.

Like everyone else, you have most likely discovered that your own success isn't easy. The good news is failure is a snap. No one is a failure at failure. It's the only thing in the entire world you can't fail at. There is shame in not failing. It means you're not trying to fail to succeed. At least when you succeed at failure you don't suck at something. Think of it as suckcess.

Mobs of triers never achieve the kind of success they dream of. A good many can't even remember their dreams and have no idea whether they are successful. There is also a preponderance of people who are successful in their dreams but not in real life, so they tend to sleep a lot.

If you're fed up with chasing the bittersweet taste of success, enjoy the lingering taste of failure combined with a breath spray.

Inspirational Words of Failure

> If you want to get better at failing, stop doing things without fail.
> Failure has no ladder to climb like with success. You don't have to be fit or have good knees.
> Going downhill is much easier than going uphill, which puts the upsides and downsides of mountains into perspective.
> When words fail you, learn another language to flounder in.
> Anyone who believes failure isn't an option never tried to lick their elbow.

Negativity Scale Checkpoint

Chapter 17: Succeed at Failure

1. The needle on my success rate status board points toward...

    a) Superstar!   _____ (5 Points)
    b) Try Harder!   _____ (10 Points)
    c) Quitter!   _____ (15 Points)
    d) Going Down!   _____ (20 Points)

2. If I were an inventor in Thomas Edison's day, while he was working on the light bulb I would have been working on...

    a) Solar panels   _____ (5 Points)
    b) Electric lamps   _____ (10 Points)
    c) Flashlights   _____ (15 Points)
    d) Matches   _____ (20 Points)

3. I have more problems with...

    a) Failure to yield   _____ (5 Points)
    b) Failure to react   _____ (10 Points)
    c) Failure to obey   _____ (15 Points)
    d) Failure to appear   _____ (20 Points)

4. I should have won more trophies over the course of my lifetime for...

    a) Passing muster   _____ (5 Points)
    b) Passing the buck   _____ (10 Points)
    c) Passing gas   _____ (15 Points)
    d) Passing bad checks   _____ (20 Points)

5. **My conclusion after conducting a complete and thorough failure assessment of myself is…**

   a) I fail to accept what fail means. _____ (5 Points)
   b) I'm going to fail to respond to this question. _____ (10 Points)
   c) If I'm good at anything, I'm accomplished at failing. _____ (15 Points)
   d) Everything around me fails, so keep your distance if you have a pacemaker. _____ (20 Points)

   Total Points, Chapter 17 _____

Things can't always get better,
but they can always get worse.

~

-18-

GRIPE, GRUMBLE, BITCH, BELLYACHE, AND KVETCH

Dissatisfied people seek satisfaction by complaining in a variety of forms. The relief they receive has been compared to desperately racing home after a barbeque to grab a piece of floss and setting free the fibrous outer shell of a chewed corn kernel stuck between two back molars.

Resentment is notorious for accumulating faster than plaque in arteries being lubed with french fry oil. Can expressing strong discontent when wallowing in resentment have the same soothing effect as medical marijuana does to reduce anxiety? No. Yet devotees of discontent believe they get a different kind of high from it.

The endless parade of bills, traffic, telemarketers with indistinguishable accents, tissues that find their way inside the washing machine and disintegrate into millions of tiny, white, clinging specks, hair in your entrée that's not yours, scurrying insects able to find an escape route the split second before you're about to clobber them, sheets that don't stay tucked under the mattress at the foot of the bed and slither up your legs in the middle of the night—giving you the willies because you think it is the insect you tried to kill getting revenge—plus run-on sentences, all take a daily toll. The only recourse is to rant, squawk, fuss, protest, and lament to your heart's content.

Medical professionals tell you complaining is not good for your mental or physical health. But when you complain about a health issue, the first thing they say is, "Run to a doctor," or "Rush to the hospital." This confirms there are aerobic exercise benefits associated with health-care-related moaning. Take all of this advice with a grain of salt or a salt substitute if you are complaining about high blood pressure.

It's time for your complaining days to wind down, anyway. You may be bewildered why there's a section called "Gripe, Grumble, Bitch, Bellyache, and Kvetch." First, it's catchy as a chapter title. Second, complaining is an unnecessary and annoying skill negative thinkers don't need to rely on.

Remember this book is training you to "find happiness through negative thinking." Putting to practice the negativity guidelines and thought processes across all of these chapters prepares you for the worst or the most preferable of the worst in every situation. The goal is to develop an it-doesn't-bother-me attitude. This alone reduces your complaining output.

There will be times when you feel the need to complain. Here's what to keep in mind when you have the urge to get something off your chest other than a barbell, mole, or bra...

Six Keys to Complaining When the Urge Hits

Key 1: Stop Pissing into the Wind
It's idiotic to grouse about stuff you have no control over, like bad weather. That's the equivalent of pissing into the wind—and afterward, anyone who has ever done this wished it was rain. Negative thinkers know there are always dark clouds hovering. Do what meteorologists do and forecast what's coming. If there's a greater than 10-percent chance of something drenching you in frustration, get out of there fast and run for cover.

Key 2: Kvetch It up a Notch
There are only two rules to remember with kvetching:

1. Whatever it is, you have it worse.
2. Whatever they do, it's not good enough.

Key 3: Diffuse Other Whiners
The quickest way to stop someone from whining your ear off is to make their whining sound even worse than they make it sound. That's right, outwhine them. When they say, "It's awful," counter with, "It's worse than awful! It's appalling, astounding, no—more like abominable!"

Key 4: Bitching Is Meant to Be a Bitch
Once the original mean bitches established themselves before long there were all kinds of bitches bitching. This includes moody bitches, insane bitches, rich bitches, stupid bitches, and f——ing bitches, to name a few. Whatever kind of bitcher you are, bitching is meant to make a point. You've hit your objective if every time your intended target sees you, Elton John's song "The Bitch Is Back" feels like it's playing in the background.

Key 5: Always Be Ready to *Grummmmble*
Grumbling is a muted way to complain—sort of like discontent in mutter mode. The best grumblers are stomachs. They can grumble about lack of food without inciting a full-blown intestinal riot. Learn from them and grummmmble away!

Key 6: Bellyache until They Get a Headache
Bellyaching oddly isn't related to stomachs unless you eat something foul, which is even more compounded if it's foul fowl. Show disapproval and bellyache until your belly isn't rubbed the wrong way.

Negativity Scale Checkpoint

Chapter 18: Gripe, Grumble, Bitch, Bellyache, and Kvetch

1. **An appropriate publication to keep pace with the frequency of my complaints is...**

    a) *Grumbler's Periodical* _____ (5 Points)
    b) *Griper's Weekly* _____ (10 Points)
    c) *Bitcher's Daily* _____ (15 Points)
    d) *Kvetcher's Chronicle* _____ (20 Points)

2. **One thing that would stand out if I ran a complaint desk is...**

    a) My incredible patience _____ (5 Points)
    b) How much aspirin I consumed _____ (10 Points)
    c) Complaints about me _____ (15 Points)
    d) All the shouting and stomping _____ (20 Points)

3. **I receive more pleasure from...**

    a) Resolving complaints _____ (5 Points)
    b) Ignoring complaints _____ (10 Points)
    c) Exaggerating complaints _____ (15 Points)
    d) Swearing out complaints _____ (20 Points)

4. **Complaints people have about me tend to...**

    a) Offend their nose _____ (5 Points)
    b) Hurt their ears _____ (10 Points)
    c) Pop their eyes _____ (15 Points)
    d) Stimulate their sweat glands _____ (20 Points)

5. **My biggest complaint about this book is it's not...**

    a) Being read to me by the author   _____ (5 Points)
    b) A multi-volume series   _____ (10 Points)
    c) Priced higher   _____ (15 Points)
    d) Being made into a feature film   _____ (20 Points)

Total Points, Chapter 18   _____

Every day is the end of something and
the beginning of the end of something else.

~

-19-

BE A BRAVE WORRIER

It took a lot of worrying to figure out how to worry. According to Lexico, the Old English origin of the word worry is "wyrgan," which translates to "strangle." In Middle English it started out meaning "to seize by the throat and tear." [9] From there unconfirmed chatter spread regarding a coincidental increase in neck-latching incidents involving anxious dogs with a lot on their minds. The meaning was later toned down to "harass," from which it evolved into "causing anxiety to." [9]

In plain English extreme worriers are taking the word too literally if they are overly concerned about either being strangled or having someone seize and tear their throat and then harass them, ultimately causing anxiety. This is probably why optimists countered with the adorable "Don't worry your pretty little head."

An actual study from the University of Cincinnati concluded 85 percent of what people worry about never happens. [10] This questionably implies that the vast majority of worried people are worrying about the wrong things.

The only way to be prepared for an unfavorable outcome is to expect one. Use the 85 percent statistic to your advantage. If you worry about winning the lottery, it could easily fall into the 85-percent-won't-happen category. Reverse the odds by worrying about losing the lottery since that's what you don't want to happen. Now you've changed the 15 percent it will happen to the 85 percent it won't happen to increase your chances it will happen. It's all a matter of simple negative math, which only a small fraction of people understand.

Countless victims die every year of heart attacks when they mistakenly worry about it being indigestion. As a result taking an antacid is about as effective as popping a couple of mini marshmallows. But they weren't nearly worried enough. A trained negative-thinking worrier would have been worried about a heart attack, angina, aortic dissection, pericarditis, indigestion, and/or gastroesophageal reflux disease. In preparation they would have had antacids, proton pump inhibitors, nitroglycerin extended-release capsules, a defibrillator, and the mini marshmallows on hand. They also would have called their doctor seven to ten times. Most importantly they might still be alive to worry about other things today.

Let's dig an even deeper hole for ourselves to look into. Most pessimists generally and specifically worry about what can go wrong. To become a more proficient negative-thinking worrier, you'll have to take it another step further and also fret about what can go right because what can go right can change and go wrong, whereas what can go wrong rarely goes right.

This creates the basis for a new formula for worrying that translates to:

> **Increase your volume of worries to cover what can go wrong as well as right.**
> +
> **Worry more about what you think won't happen so it will have a better chance of happening.**
> =
> **Be better prepared to survive each day with minimal damage to your well-being and body organs.**

Positive thinkers are confident everything will turn out fine and throw caution to the wind. Leading wind energy whizzes are baffled as to why anyone would throw caution into moving air in the first place or what the proper technique for propelling it through the atmosphere is. It is even more challenging when it's not windy, yet optimists are 100 percent convinced all their problems will eventually blow over. No one knows where the wind gusts the caution nonworriers throw around. It doesn't appear to be Chicago. For connoisseurs of negative thinking, all of this is something to worry about.

There's also no point in worrying yourself sick, especially if you're worried about getting sick. This defeats the purpose of worrying about it, which is why you should worry more about not getting sick. Should you not get sick, at least you'll have evidence your immune system is functioning at its peak.

Never believe anyone who says, "No worries!" They're not worried enough to trust. Keep in mind that worrying is the first cousin of anxiety, the brother-in-law of fear, and the oldest son of panic. This clarifies why there are families of worriers.

Stop trying to take the worry out of things. Focus on putting worry into things. Doing it the right way is the trademark of a brave worrier.

Negativity Scale Checkpoint

Chapter 19: Be a Brave Worrier

1. After looking deep into my eyes, you could tell I'd be more likely to say…

    a) "What, me worry?" _____ (5 Points)
    b) "Let me worry about it." _____ (10 Points)
    c) "You better be worried!" _____ (15 Points)
    d) "Can't you see I'm so worried I'm covered in warts?" _____ (20 Points)

2. When I kick into worry mode, the experience is similar to watching…

    a) Ballet _____ (5 Points)
    b) Blindfolded archery _____ (10 Points)
    c) Playing in traffic _____ (15 Points)
    d) Squirrel wrestling _____ (20 Points)

3. If you were in my shoes, you would be more worried about…

    a) Dragging your feet _____ (5 Points)
    b) Putting my foot in your mouth _____ (10 Points)
    c) Walking into trouble _____ (15 Points)
    d) Getting booted out of places _____ (20 Points)

4. Worry beads—ha! I need something stronger, like a…

    a) Worry stress ball _____ (5 Points)
    b) Worry chew toy _____ (10 Points)
    c) Worry hair extension _____ (15 Points)
    d) Worry sledgehammer _____ (20 Points)

5. **If a worry lab performed a full exam on me, the final report would reveal…**

   a) I'm uneasy about uncertainty   _____ (5 Points)
   b) I'm disturbed by distress   _____ (10 Points)
   c) I'm wallowing in worriment   _____ (15 Points)
   d) I'm plagued by perplexity   _____ (20 Points)

Total Points, Chapter 19   _____

Like all good things, all bad things
eventually come to an end.

∼

-20-

DON'T UNDERESTIMATE UNDERACHIEVING

Parents who don't claim their children are overachievers are rarer than termites allergic to wood. They're also either blatantly mistaken or something went terribly wrong for their kid after puberty. The typical child grows into an adult who is no more than average. An enormous percentage need a referral from the scarecrow to the wizard, hoping to uncover why they're not the overachieving geniuses their parents told them they were.

Underachievers unfairly get a bum rap. So what if they achieve less than expected? Who sets the bar anyway, and how do we know they're not setting it at a bar? Have you ever met anyone with a degree in bar setting? If you did, and they didn't meet your expectations, would you still try to meet theirs? What if the closest they've ever personally come to achieving anything involving a bar is using a bar of soap or having a bar mitzvah? The whole idea of setting bars should be barred. Even those who are behind bars would vote to get rid of them.

Awards are prized possessions. Scads of distinguished notables have won lifetime achievement awards. In the name of equal time, there was recent buzz circulating about television networks launching lifetime underachievement awards. It was scrapped when executives had an epiphany and feared they themselves could be nominated.

Nowadays in youth sports, everyone gets a trophy. They're all considered overachievers—even the uncoordinated ones who look at a ball and pull an eye muscle. Wait until they go into the real world and discover everyone doesn't get a raise at the same time simply for showing up to work every day.

There are varying degrees of expectations—high, low, and no. Positive thinkers believe they can achieve anything. Meeting or exceeding expectations at a high level is difficult to sustain on an ongoing basis. It opens the door to frequent failures, frustrations, fiascos, and flies. This is why you're better off with low or no expectations. Presto! Then anything you do is an achievement.

According to nameless bookies, Las Vegas oddsmakers handicap levels of achievement by determining the differential in the over/under spread. This includes: overachievers versus underachievers, overdogs versus underdogs, overperformers versus underperformers, and who accomplishes more in overwear versus underwear. Any way you look at it, the under group comes out at the bottom, unless there's an upset. The good news for negative thinkers is they are always aware of anything with the potential to upset them.

Tests are another barometer of achievement. It's hazy why a scientific weather instrument has anything to do with testing. While test takers are under pressure, it's seldom barometric pressure. Lots of test takers come up short. The only tests a good portion of them can pass are blood tests. If someone can overachieve at needle-to-arm-to-test-tube phlebotomy lab results, it doesn't guarantee they're going to do as well with blood clotting, blood poisoning, or mixing a Bloody Mary.

Some extremely capable people underachieve while other highly incapable people overachieve. The important thing to remember is that everything you achieve is an achievement—whether it's something or nothing. Otherwise why would anyone say, "You've achieved nothing"? It only proves that nothing is something. Learning all of this is a colossal achievement in itself.

There are gazillions of opportunities for underachievers to find their places and pursue happiness. Take politics for example. CNN reports that Congress's approval rating hasn't hit 30 percent in ten years. [11]

Ineffective politicians keep getting elected, despite a clear perception of underachieving. Tons of professional athletes turn out to be busts and still make millions. Meanwhile women of all shapes and sizes have achieved fame by flaunting outstanding busts. In the music business, a long list of artists will forever be remembered for single hits. This illustrates why overachieving is overrated. Achieving something once is often enough. Ask anyone who's come back to life after being pronounced dead.

There are unhappy overachievers as well as happy underachievers. Keep in mind overachieving at underachieving is much better than underachieving at overachieving, which is something everyone either needs to understand or overstand.

Negativity Scale Checkpoint

Chapter 20: Don't Underestimate Underachieving

1. As far as overachievers and underachievers go, Las Vegas oddsmakers would classify me as...

    a) A natural over _____ (5 Points)
    b) A semi-over/semi-under _____ (10 Points)
    c) An authentic under _____ (15 Points)
    d) An over-and-out under _____ (20 Points)

2. Forget the Midas touch! Anything I touch turns to...

    a) Cheering _____ (5 Points)
    b) Nodding _____ (10 Points)
    c) Heckling _____ (15 Points)
    d) Something you wouldn't touch with a ten-foot pole _____ (20 Points)

3. It would not be a lie if my family engraved on my gravestone, "Here lies...

    a) a doer." _____ (5 Points)
    b) a redoer." _____ (10 Points)
    c) an undoer." _____ (15 Points)
    d) a do nothinger." _____ (20 Points)

4. Ever since I can remember, I believed I could achieve...

    a) Immortality _____ (5 Points)
    b) Almost anything _____ (10 Points)
    c) The minimum required _____ (15 Points)
    d) Total insignificance _____ (20 Points)

5. **Anyone who has known me my entire life will confirm I've been an…**

   a) Overachieving child and
      overachieving adult   _____ (5 Points)
   b) Underachieving child and
      overachieving adult   _____ (10 Points)
   c) Overachieving child and
      underachieving adult   _____ (15 Points)
   d) Underachieving child and
      underachieving adult   _____ (20 Points)

Total Points, Chapter 20   _____

Unless you work for NASA,
don't shoot for the moon.

-21-

KNOW MOTIVATION

I don't feel like writing this chapter. It's as simple as that.

Negativity Scale Checkpoint

Chapter 21: Know Motivation

1. If I used pennies to represent all the activities I'm not motivated to do on most days, in a year they would come closer to filling up a...

    a) Shoe box   _____ (5 Points)
    b) Bathtub   _____ (10 Points)
    c) Green dumpster   _____ (15 Points)
    d) Wide-body aircraft _____ (20 Points)

2. To add up the hours I've lost to being unmotivated in the last three years, I'd need...

    a) An abacus   _____ (5 Points)
    b) A calculator   _____ (10 Points)
    c) An accounting firm   _____ (15 Points)
    d) Mathematicians from the space program _____ (20 Points)

3. When it comes to capturing my level of motivation, the brand that said it best is...

    a) Nike:
       Just do it.   _____ (5 Points)
    b) Vodaphone:
       Make the most of now.   _____ (10 Points)
    c) McDonald's:
       You deserve a break today.   _____ (15 Points)
    d) Harley-Davidson:
       Screw it. Let's ride.   _____ (20 Points)

4. My attitude when I feel unmotivated can be positioned as…

   a) Not now   _____ (5 Points)
   b) Not listening   _____ (10 Points)
   c) Not happening   _____ (15 Points)
   d) Not ever!   _____ (20 Points)

5. The incentive I think would have the best chance of motivating me to get off my butt is…

   a) A pat on the back   _____ (5 Points)
   b) A gift card   _____ (10 Points)
   c) Begging me to do it   _____ (15 Points)
   d) Snow in Fiji   _____ (20 Points)

Total Points, Chapter 21   _____

A big knock on opportunity is it's
not an equal opportunity for all.

∼

-22-

IMPATIENCE IS THE VIRTUE

It's not easy to remain calm while slowly being pulled along as ho-hum, hectic, horrible, or happy events unfold. Wait it out. Snore. Snore. Snore. Positive-thinking virtuosos blew it on the patience virtue. This isn't the time for standby mode. Ticktock, ticktock. It's when you want to be impatient.

Waiting isn't always worth the wait. Situations frequently get worse while you endure for hours to decades. Optimists dissolve frustration by convincing themselves, "Good things come to those who wait." Meanwhile everything leads to deadlock. It's the equivalent of rigor mortis for the living.

Being patient isn't as simple as Simon says. Anonymous sources who like being told what to do reveal that Simon loses his patience repeatedly. Simon says a command; they do the opposite and drop out of his game. At first it was cute. After a while Simon cracked. That's why he never invented another game. This is the problem with patience—it's hard to find and easy to lose.

The gold standard is having the patience of a saint. It was a stunning revelation when first announced. Centuries later it had a resurgence and got unruly when folks in New Orleans took it to include members of their professional football team. At the time the Saints were on a serious losing streak. Shockingly, unsuspecting pedestrians were being tackled everywhere from the French Quarter all the way to Mississippi and chunks of Alabama.

Patient optimists diddle away time thinking good thoughts. Impatient pessimists judge situations more thoroughly by sniffing out potential problem areas. Positive thinkers use "I can't wait" as an expression of excitement. Negative thinkers alter the delivery to "I. Can't. Wait." The impatience behind it is a driving force to get where you're going—or not going—faster.

The standard you should adopt is having the impatience of a demanding mother. They don't wait for anything. Clean your room now. Eat now. Go to sleep now. Study now. Let's go now. What if you stall? You're grounded now.

The urgency of Mom's demands is mighty motivating. You did what had to be done because her impatience is the difference between now and ow. Alternatively if someone has a patient mom, they might have spent their entire childhood living in a pigsty, always hungry, suffering from lack of sleep, being late for everything, and still waiting to graduate.

This condensed ten-step guide will help you develop a higher level of impatience. There were originally fifty-two steps, but even patient readers wouldn't have the patience to go through them all.

Ten Steps to Increasing Impatience in a Hurry

Step 1: No Waiting—Tom Petty got it right when he sang, "The waiting is the hardest part." The Rolling Stones also nailed it with, "...and time waits for no one, and it won't wait for me." [12] Rock on, but don't wait on.

Step 2: Never Fall for That Line—Whether you stand on line or in line, get off the line. Use impatience to get whatever you need somewhere else. Always make sure your impatience is shorter than the line.

Step 3: Make Gratification Instant—Patience gives you delayed gratification. Have you ever had a boss or client who said, "No rush"? Exactly. Get your gratification now, without delay.

Step 4: Never Lose Your Patience Again—If you don't have patience, it's impossible to lose it. You never hear of anyone losing their impatience.

Step 5: Sweat the Big and Small Stuff—Perspiration pushes people to move faster in two ways:

a) They sense you're under pressure or stressed and make more of an effort to keep things moving.

b) Once they see pit stains and craniofacial hyperhidrosis, they want to dispatch quicker and get away from you.

Step 6: Don't Go *Network* Mad—You've pushed patience too far if you're yelling out a window, "I'm mad as hell, and I'm not going to take this anymore!" [13] Know when to turn persistence into resistance. Pinpoint what you don't have patience for before you go nuts and bail long before someone comes to fit you for a straitjacket.

Step 7: Connect Your Pulse to Your Impulse—Put your index and middle fingers on your carotid artery to the side of your windpipe. Do this at intervals throughout any impulse you have. When your patience wears thin, follow your heart and move to your pulse's faster beat.

Step 8: End Patience Testing—This is a trap positive thinkers fall into. Never let people test your patience. See how things change by allowing them to test your impatience. They might be sorry they did, but you won't.

Step 9: Impatience Is Easy to Grasp—Forget practicing patience. Impatience doesn't require any practice.

Step 10: Get Your Way—The way to get your way is to get whatever is in your way out of your way. As a demanding mom would say, "Do it now!"

Negativity Scale Checkpoint

Chapter 22: Impatience Is the Virtue

1. Ask me to do something, and there's a good chance I'll get to it…

    a) Now or soon   _____ (5 Points)
    b) Later or eventually   _____ (10 Points)
    c) Who knows or it's hard to say   _____ (15 Points)
    d) Don't hold your breath, or it's never gonna happen   _____ (20 Points)

2. The sound of me being impatient resembles…

    a) Hmm, hmm, hmm   _____ (5 Points)
    b) Tap, tap, tap   _____ (10 Points)
    c) Hwooo, hwooo, hwooo   _____ (15 Points)
    d) Grrr, grrr, grrr   _____ (20 Points)

3. The first thought that pops into my mind when I take on any endeavor is…

    a) "Let's get it right."   _____ (5 Points)
    b) "Let's get it on."   _____ (10 Points)
    c) "Let's get it together."   _____ (15 Points)
    d) "Let's get it over with."   _____ (20 Points)

4. One clear sign I've lost my patience is…

    a) My eyes roll   _____ (5 Points)
    b) My mind races   _____ (10 Points)
    c) Doors slam   _____ (15 Points)
    d) Walls get new holes   _____ (20 Points)

5. **In the Impatient Winter Olympics, the event I'd win a gold medal for is the…**

    a) Bite-my-tongue biathlon _____ (5 Points)
    b) Lip curling competition _____ (10 Points)
    c) Rolling-head bobsled _____ (15 Points)
    d) Going-downhill-fast skiing _____ (20 Points)

Total Points, Chapter 22 _____

Positive thinkers think they can see the invisible.
Negative thinkers think they are invisible.

~

-23-

HIT THEM RIGHT BETWEEN THE LIES

They can be big or small. They'll pop up anywhere. If you're on the receiving end, you either get the shaft or stiffed. Eventually they reach a climax. The culprits are ding-dongs, ding-a-lings, and putzes. We're talking about lies.

There are all kinds of liars. You don't have to be board certified in dentistry to spot someone who lies through their teeth. In a controversial, jaw-dropping, unheard-of report, nine out of ten dentists agreed the world would be a much better place if lying caused tooth decay and candy didn't. The other 10 percent couldn't accept what it would mean for Halloween. They preferred multiple cavities to the scary reality of kids knocking on doors and receiving sweets from homeowners, in or out of costume, missing real teeth.

Lying is a reflex action for compulsive liars. They spit out lies faster than spitters spit out spit at other passengers on New York City subway trains. Make it a point to avoid anyone who spits out anything when they talk or listen.

There are also natural-born liars. Watch out for them. They consider it a blessing to have received that gift over the gift natural-born killers got. It gets extra confusing with liars who think they're telling the truth and don't even believe themselves.

It's easy to be fooled when a lie is disguised as the truth, or the truth is disguised as a lie. For some people it's hard enough to figure out if a president is disguised as a Russian agent. We've all been fooled more than once by someone seemingly honorable who was disguised as a human.

Once someone lies you can bet another lie is coming. Lying has no place in negative thinking. The only time a lie is acceptable is when you own two or more dogs and they're sleeping. Let them lie.

The best protections against lying are your negative-sensing senses. Negative thinking focuses on foreseeing and preparing for the whole truth—from lousy to wretched. Developing the ability to transform yourself into a lie detector is critical for this to happen. These pointers will help you better identify deceit:

Learn to Smell a Liar
Most noses can smell a rat. Thanks to deodorant, sniffing out a practiced liar requires a different approach. Even Nostrildamus couldn't do it. An effective way to study the full range of telltale signs someone is lying is to spend at least seventy-five to one hundred hours watching videos of politicians.

Use the Laughing Lie Trick
If you suspect someone is lying, let out a laugh and jokingly reply, "You're lying." See how they defend their story. It's a terrific way to accuse someone of lying without them feeling incriminated. For variety mix it with, "That's not true!" or "You made it up!" or the all-time hilarious classic, "Liar, liar, pants on fire!"

Differentiate Small Talk versus Lie Talk
It would be awkward to connect whomever you're with to a polygraph machine. But polygraphers ask feeler questions first, and so can you. Try basic questions like, "It's driving me crazy; do you know the capital of Montana?" If they say, "Billings," it doesn't mean they're lying. They may be bad at geography or poorly educated since the correct answer is Helena. Either way observe their body language during the setup questions and compare it to what their body says during tougher questions.

Trust What You're Hearing Is a Lie
Beware of yappers who talk to nipples instead of eyeballs. Listen for insincere clues like "to be honest" or "believe me." Watch out for opera acts featuring the hit aria, "Me-Me-Me-Me." Other fabrications are performed as a song and dance. Lying comes in many forms. All can be heard, sung, or lip-synched.

Look Out for False Positives and True Negatives
When someone says something positive that's untrue, it's a false positive. It's also possible to think someone is lying when it's the truth, which results in a true negative. Keep in mind you have a fifty-fifty shot at being wrong with true-false scenarios. Mix in multiple choice options and evaluate those answers too.

> A liar has one enemy—anyone who questions their lies.

Negativity Scale Checkpoint

Chapter 23: Hit Them Right between the Lies

1. If my nose grew every time I lied, by the end of a typical week it would extend from my face...

    a) Out an inch or two _____ (5 Points)
    b) To my fingertips _____ (10 Points)
    c) About a mile _____ (15 Points)
    d) Over the border to the next-closest country _____ (20 Points)

2. My last memorable lie was created for something...

    a) I didn't do _____ (5 Points)
    b) I did do _____ (10 Points)
    c) I don't remember _____ (15 Points)
    d) No comment based on the grounds it could incriminate me _____ (20 Points)

3. The movie title that best describes my lying skills is...

    a) *Where the Truth Lies* _____ (5 Points)
    b) *White Lie* _____ (10 Points)
    c) *Liar Liar* _____ (15 Points)
    d) *Dangerous Lies* _____ (20 Points)

4. The penalty for lying to me is...

    a) Tickle them until they pee _____ (5 Points)
    b) Forgive them but don't forget _____ (10 Points)
    c) Report them _____ (15 Points)
    d) Ruin them on social media _____ (20 Points)

5. **If I were on the television show *To Tell the Truth,* the panel would conclude…**

   a) I'm a terrific bluffer _____ (5 Points)
   b) I like to stretch the truth _____ (10 Points)
   c) If I ever went on trial, I'd be convicted of perjury _____ (15 Points)
   d) I could have made a fortune as a con artist _____ (20 Points)

   Total Points, Chapter 23 _____

Optimists believe in hope and joy.
When hope runs out, they never jump for joy.

∽

-24-

YOU HAVE MY SYMPATHY

There's a lot to learn about sympathy from the dearly departed. Family, friends, acquaintances, and cemetery squatters say the nicest things, even if they don't believe it or mean it. It's hard to duplicate those kinds of heartfelt sympathies in real life. Alive corpses who are dead on their feet have proven this.

It isn't fair to wait until the touching words, "You have my sympathy," followed by other tear-jerking reflections, are conveyed after you're gone. It does you little good to not hear it once you have a new forwarding address where there's no texting, phone service, or underground café to get a much-needed ego massage.

If only you could figure out how to get people to say the things they write in sympathy cards while you're still breathing. Well, you can—and if you act now, we'll include this cozy coffin pillow, celestial comforter, and 30-percent-off coupon on either wings or horns—for when your time does come.

It may sound like a far-fetched concept; however, getting the sympathy you deserve is attainable without waiting. But wait! You don't want the everyday self-generated sympathies that get people feeling sorry for you. "I'm the victim" and "Woe is me" are sadfishing expeditions, which make for pathetic, not sympathetic, catches of the day. Don't waste your time trying to validate your senses of inferiority, insecurity, inadequacy, inconsequentiality, and intimacy. Instead explore other ways of getting sympathy without throwing yourself a pity party, which sucks anyway because no one brings gifts.

There are different kinds of sympathies. All are connected to real, imaginary, or fake feelings and emotions. Let's explore how to generate genuine sympathy that's to die for:

Dive into the Deep End—Winning a person's deepest sympathy is the ultimate grand prize. All you have to do is rip someone's heart out. Figuratively is much less messy than literally.

Create Guilt for Deepest Sympathy
Send your intended target on a guilt trip. Don't show mercy even if you see tears in the whites of their bloodshot eyes. These guilty pleasure motivators should help.

> "Why did you promise never to do that again and do it anyway? Do you think I have amnesia?"
> "When you look in the mirror, are you the fairest of them all? Never mind. I'll ask your mirror."
> "Are you able to sleep with yourself, or do you prefer to be alone?"

Apply for an Extension—When someone extends their sympathy, stretch it further. They'll have to feel you without touching, although it can be a bonus if you find them attractive and they do have sympathetic hands.

Elicit Empathy for Extended Sympathy
Get your audience to feel with you, not for you. These provocative, touchy-feely thought provokers connect your feelings to theirs:

> "How do you feel about how I'm feeling?"
> "Is your inner gut as nauseated as mine?"
> "You do feel me; it's like we're twins."

In or Out?—People show their sympathetic sides in many ways. These are some of the ins and outs.

Solicit Support for In Sympathy
To get someone in sympathy with you, take them along for the ride to experience whatever you're going through. Use these call-for-help tempters to draw them in:

> "This will be awful with your help, but it's going to be dreadful without it."
> "I know I'm asking a lot, but if I only ask a little, you wouldn't do it, right?"
> "Can you do this with me, or do I have to beg?"

Out of sympathy only becomes a challenging obstacle if they are truly out of it...

Transfer Power for Out of Sympathy
Instead of going through it with you, urge others to go through it for you. Try these direct lay-it-on-the-liners:

> "Would you do it for a steak dinner?"
> "Can you be my guardian angel on this one?"
> "I need a superhero. Can you rescue me as soon as possible?"

It would be a shame not to enjoy afterlife sympathy during this life. Don't let people bury their feelings to the point you can't hear them until they bury you. Once you grasp the guidelines of gaining and generating sympathy, you'll be better equipped to get some without the boohoos.

Negativity Scale Checkpoint

Chapter 24: You Have My Sympathy

1. **If I were a fountain of sympathy, I'd be...**

    a) Flowing strong   _____ (5 Points)
    b) Slowly trickling   _____ (10 Points)
    c) Clogged   _____ (15 Points)
    d) Out of order   _____ (20 Points)

2. **I have more sympathy for...**

    a) Animals   _____ (5 Points)
    b) Movie characters   _____ (10 Points)
    c) Myself   _____ (15 Points)
    d) The devil   _____ (20 Points)

3. **When someone I know needs a sympathetic ear, I'll...**

    a) Bend over backward   _____ (5 Points)
    b) Pretend to listen but think about other things   _____ (10 Points)
    c) Feel like ants are in my pants   _____ (15 Points)
    d) Tell them I have an earache   _____ (20 Points)

4. **If a TV remote control were connected to my feelings of sympathy, during touching moments it would...**

    a) Suffer a battery drain   _____ (5 Points)
    b) Blast the volume   _____ (10 Points)
    c) Quickly change channels   _____ (15 Points)
    d) Turn off the TV   _____ (20 Points)

5. I admit I'm tempted to get more sympathy by...

    a) Praying for it   _____ (5 Points)
    b) Asking for it   _____ (10 Points)
    c) Begging for it   _____ (15 Points)
    d) Paying for it   _____ (20 Points)

Total Points, Chapter 24   _____

Winners have more to lose than losers.

~

-25-

MANAGE ANGER LIKE A VAMPIRE

Anger is brewing. You can feel your blood begin to boil. This is where studies of vampires, the leading authorities on boiling blood, have yielded invaluable information with biting insights.

Vampires know better than anyone the dangers of sticking your neck out when emotions run high. All of the bad things medical experts attribute to anger don't apply to vamps. That's why they never die from stress, heart attacks, or brain bursts. In fact they sleep calmly and are crackerjacks at controlling blood pressure levels. The only thing that has been known to do them in is a bad experience at a stakehouse.

Even the skin of vampires is amazing, and it's not only because they stay out of the sun. Humans have made vampire facials fabulously popular. Many say no other facial pales in comparison. All of this proves vampires know how to face anger, yet they refuse to let anger show on their faces.

You never hear anything in the news about angry vampires lashing out by protesting or looting blood banks. It's like they have an on/off anger management switch to restrain them from going batshit crazy.

Vampires snicker at our primitive methods for controlling anger. Count Dracula in particular understood why counting to ten in an attempt to defuse a potential meltdown isn't always easy or effective. Counting may also be adding fuel to the fire since an astounding 93 percent of Americans report experiencing some level of math anxiety. [14] Angerologists considered changing this numeric temper suppression aid to reciting the alphabet letters *a* through *j*. Unfortunately vocabulary test scores in America are also dropping. As a result people risk getting stuck on the way to *j* and remaining rage bound if they follow the exercise to the letter.

Controlled breathing is another technique recommended by mad scientists. Breathe deeply and imagine relaxing things. You're floating in the ocean. Soothing waves gently rock you. The sun feels delicious on your body. Hey, is that a surfboard or a shark? Shark! You're swimming as fast as you can. You've got a cramp. The shark is closing in. Whew! It's a surfboard. You have to pee really bad. Too late; not anymore. You've made it to the beach. Harpoon-like needles shoot out from the tentacle of a jellyfish and inject the bottom of your foot with venom. Your skin feels prickly. Now it's burning. So much for trying to achieve a peaceful state. Your train of thought has been derailed. The anger is back in full force and you're thinking, "Whom can I yell at other than the jellyfish?"

For most human mammals, being angry and trying not to breathe heavily like a bronchialsaurus is like trying to pat your head and rub your belly in opposite directions simultaneously. Not everyone has the kind of windpipe willpower and metacarpal muscle-movement coordination to pull this off. After two deep breaths, you still want to go flat-out berserko.

One little-known technique for dissolving anger is repeatedly scratching the side of your chin at high speed like dogs do. There are two reasons this works: it's shockingly amusing, and it freezes the other party in disbelief. If you are able to simulate foaming at the mouth, it's a big perk.

Another infrequently promoted course of anger control is blinking as fast as you can until you forget what you were angry about. This procedure evolved from the historic hairy eyeball phenomenon. Be sure to rest your eyes afterward to ensure they don't continue to roll around in their sockets, resulting in vertigo, which—like anger—can make your head spin.

When all else fails, this trick will do the trick: let's say you're going at it with your mom. Stay calm and respond monotonously in monotone to everything she says with, "Yes, Mom. Yes, Mom. Yes, Mom.

Yes, Mom. Yes, Mom." **Warning:** This plan of attack will send even the most patient of people over the edge. Do not try this with anyone when sharp objects or firearms are anywhere nearby.

The entire concept of negative anger management offers a new way of approaching and refocusing anger. Managing anger in itself implies you have anger that needs managing. When it's mismanaged you get madder than after the hundredth telemarketing call informing you, "We've detected your PC has a virus." A terrific way to practice staying calm is to let the telemarketer talk. Keep responding with comments like "Uh-huh" and "Tell me more." After twenty minutes say, "Wait a minute. I have a Mac."

Negative thinking gives you the upper hand by stifling anger before it takes off. The good news is you don't have to become a vampire and guzzle gallons of blood or beet juice to manage anger. When scrutinizing situations, negative thinkers instinctively imagine every scenario down to the unimaginable. As previously established, when you expect the worst, you're less upset when it happens. Disappointment is already built in. Potential suffering has been analyzed. Most if not all of the negatives have been calculated. Anger is kept in check when you don't count on anything good happening. You can't count on that when you count to ten with your teeth clenched so hard they're receding into your sinuses. Originally they wanted agitated people to count to one hundred. Somewhere around fifty-six…fifty-seven…fifty-eight…someone was inevitably on the receiving end of everything from a wedgie to being chased by a kook dressed like Thor swinging a hammer.

Instead of getting mad, use negative thinking as your on/off anger management switch. Flip it and turn off your emotions. Allow the negativity to flow through your veins. Visualize your blood desensitizing and blocking hemoglobin from oxidizing to combust with hydrogen and carbon dioxide before you reach your boiling point. Tune others out until you can't hear them, see them, or feel them when you can't stand them. Once you set your negative radar to high alert like vampires, you won't be driven batty anymore.

Negativity Scale Checkpoint

Chapter 25: Manage Anger like a Vampire

1. **If a real anger guidance expert (RAGE) analyzed my anger, they'd say it was being managed now by...**

    a) People with lockjaw _____ (5 Points)
    b) Clowns _____ (10 Points)
    c) Primal screamers _____ (15 Points)
    d) MMA fighters _____ (20 Points)

2. **In terms of fishing for answers about my anger, I have more in common with a...**

    a) Grunt _____ (5 Points)
    b) Blowfish _____ (10 Points)
    c) Bullhead _____ (15 Points)
    d) Cutthroat trout _____ (20 Points)

3. **It would be beneficial for anyone around me when I'm angry to be above average at...**

    a) Running _____ (5 Points)
    b) Hiding _____ (10 Points)
    c) Ducking _____ (15 Points)
    d) Praying _____ (20 Points)

4. **The natural disaster my anger most resembles when it strikes is...**

    a) A flood of mixed emotions _____ (5 Points)
    b) A slow-burn wildfire _____ (10 Points)
    c) An avalanche of insults _____ (15 Points)
    d) An earth-under-your-feet quake _____ (20 Points)

5. If a tempermometer existed, my reading this year would be hovering around...

   a) Normal   _____ (5 Points)
   b) Deep freeze   _____ (10 Points)
   c) Sky high   _____ (15 Points)
   d) Burning hot and ready to explode   _____ (20 Points)

Total Points, Chapter 25   _____

Don't worry about finishing what you can't start.

∼

-26-

STOP MAKING EXCUSES FOR MAKING EXCUSES

Not all excuses are excusable. The challenge is crafting the right excuse. Ari called in sick to work. He claimed he caught a bacterial infection from his turtles, Sal and Monella. Maybelline cancelled plans with several friends. Her horoscope said to avoid people because Libra's seventh house was a mess, thanks to activity involving Mars. Moira cancelled her hair salon appointment. Her excuse: "Too much of my hair has been falling out lately, so I need to conserve what's left."

When you hear, "Stop making excuses," the reason is you gave someone a ridiculous excuse. There's a jagged line between good and bad excuses. A good one offers a valid reason because it stands to reason. Bad excuses can't be reasoned, for good reason. It comes down to if there's a rhyme or reason for whether the excuse is one you can deduce or consider abstruse.

When we were youngsters, our parents made excuses for us. They would send notes to school like, "Please excuse Octavius from swimming today. He has an open boil in a spot his bathing suit won't cover." Or they would use us as an excuse to cancel plans. "Eugenia has a fever of 102.8 and she's been in an ice bath for forty minutes." In reality her temperature was 99.1 and she hasn't had any kind of a bath in three days.

An excuse is nothing more than an escape route to get out of something you can't, won't, or don't want to do. Negative thinkers formulate excuses as a necessary evil for avoiding potential obstacles, misfortunes, and calamities. Lame excuses like "I don't feel like waiting on that long line for the roller coaster" are wishy washy. Success depends on believable reasoning, created to convince the other person to agree with you. For instance, "If I go on the roller coaster, there's no question you'll spend the rest of the afternoon covered in vomit." In a blink the subject is closed. This approach works as long as it's believable, even with a retched excuse.

Excuses only work as a get-out-of-doing-something-awful card before whatever happens does happen. Once it happens it's too late to make it unhappen. Your alibi may get you into hot water at work, piss off a friend, or lead to a significant other becoming a discus thrower and hurling a robot vacuum at your head. But if it gets you out of doing something you don't want to do—hallelujah!

Negative thinking gives you the advantage of delivering solid excuses conceived to work at the ideal time—prior to the point of negative impact. Positive thinkers can't possibly see this point. They are too positive and unable to envision all the potential things that could go wrong. Consequently they can't develop the excuses necessary for whatever may require an excuse. They proceed anyway thinking everything will turn out fine. When things go south or even north, west, and east, they have no direction, no credible hypothesis, and no way out.

A big misconception about excuses is you have to find one. Actually they find you. Look no further than right in front of your eyes without crossing them, or they won't line up. When negative thinking is in full flow, you're already analyzing whether you need an excuse before an excuse is necessary.

One type of excuse to avoid is "my" excuses like "Excuse my French; I'm German" or "Excuse my father; he's a farter." Every person consists of three people: me, myself, and I. "My" excuses feel like you're only trying to excuse one of you or complicate the excuse by including a relative or friend.

Excuses have been misused, abused, and confused. They've been twisted into fishy stories for concealing misdeeds and blurted out as justifications that can't be justified. Massive numbers of excuse makers never learned how to come up with good excuses, which is inexcusable. Here's how to rectify that:

Effective Excuse Execution

> Compile the pros and cons of a situation. Eliminate all the pros. Anything you want to make an excuse for will be in the con column. Conprende?
> To bail out of a situation, develop your excuse based on one or more of the negatives and stick to it like the tiny water bacterium *Caulobacter crescentus*.
> If you proceed with a situation, the negatives should outweigh the positives. This is the true test of whether you want to do something badly enough. Otherwise brainstorm an excuse with yourself and get out of it.
> Once you commit it's too late for excuses. You'll need a valid reason for anything that arises for which you would have initially needed an excuse. There is no chapter in this book dedicated to reasoning since there are too many people you can't reason with.

Negativity Scale Checkpoint

Chapter 26: Stop Making Excuses for Making Excuses

1. My attitude toward excuses has always been...

    a) "I don't make excuses." _____ (5 Points)
    b) "I'm sick of your excuses." _____ (10 Points)
    c) "I've got no excuse for all the excuses I make." _____ (15 Points)
    d) "I can't answer because I have a pistachio nut stuck in my upper esophageal sphincter." _____ (20 Points)

2. I could use a good excuse for...

    a) Getting out of ruts _____ (5 Points)
    b) Getting out of trouble _____ (10 Points)
    c) Getting out of dodge _____ (15 Points)
    d) Getting out of bed _____ (20 Points)

3. My excuses tend to...

    a) Evolve and expand _____ (5 Points)
    b) Sizzle and fizzle _____ (10 Points)
    c) Backfire and boomerang _____ (15 Points)
    d) Horrify and haunt _____ (20 Points)

4. When I look in the mirror, I have no excuse why...

    a) I look so hot _____ (5 Points)
    b) There aren't more of me _____ (10 Points)
    c) I appear so far away _____ (15 Points)
    d) Anyone wouldn't love me _____ (20 Points)

5. **If I'm accused of making excuses, my excuse is…**

   a) I did it my way   _____ (5 Points)
   b) It was downhill all the way   _____ (10 Points)
   c) That's the way the wind
      was blowing   _____ (15 Points)
   d) The Lord works in mysterious ways   _____ (20 Points)

Total Points, Chapter 26   _____

One criticize doesn't fit all.

~

-27-

YOU WANT YOUR BACK AGAINST THE WALL

Staggering numbers of individuals don't allow anything on their back other than a backpack or the firm hands of a masseuse or masseur. When *dosha*-balancing, penetrating Ayurvedic body oils are palpitated deep into your tight trapezius, sore latissimus dorsi, and rigid rhomboids, they untie toxin-filled knots. It's exactly what the body kneads to relax as you float away on a sea of self-absorbed negative cogitation. Hopefully you enjoyed this pleasant meditative diversion, but let's get back on track to what this chapter is meant to be about.

One unintentional thing throngs of people do have on their back is a target. Negative thinkers should avoid any type of target other than the store. Gun range and archery targets aren't good for backs either, due to the risks of having someone shooting body-piercing ammunition at you from behind. While body piercings are popular, the ones that go in and out of your entire body or get lodged within vital organs are unadvisable.

Negative thinkers should block out targets and go with a wall. Any kind of wall will do, although brick walls are strong and solid. People built like a brick shithouse can attest to this.

Psychologically when your back is against the wall in real time, the situation is desperate or dire with few or no options. By intentionally choosing to align your back to a wall, you're able to see things from the most optimal negative angles. Then when you get hit by an inevitable ton of bricks, you can respond to whoever's behind it brick by brick. Another fun benefit is if you don't feel like talking to someone, you can make them feel like they're talking to a brick wall without turning your back on them. If you want to mess with them even more, ask if they'd like to bang their head against you.

Negative senses are heightened with your symbolic wall in place. You'll push further and fight harder, yet you'll be unfazed by the negativity surrounding you since you weren't expecting anything positive to materialize anyway. Positive thinkers often feel walled in when struggling to wiggle out of frustrating or stressful back-to-the-wall situations. Pessimists never think this and have nothing to lose since they're used to climbing walls.

Negative thinkers should also actively seek out backers. These are godsends who are always saying, "I've got your back." Whenever you hear anyone say it, do everything you can to make them a friend. A backer offers invaluable protection from someone who voluntarily wants to watch your back at no cost. It's the kind of back support everyone needs. You'll never find an orthopedist willing to do that.

Another type of friend worth being on the lookout for is anyone willing to give you the shirt off their back, especially if they have a great chest. Hold them to it too. It's not only a great way to ensure other eyes are looking out for you; it's also a terrific way to expand your wardrobe.

A series of negative situations often follow one another. They can spiral to the point where something snaps, including you. Unrecognized scholars in the Middle East refer to this phenomenon as the straw that broke the camel's back. Downbeat desert dwellers figured out from experience how critical it is to avoid loading camels past their capacity and why it's a terrible idea to let them drink from straws when they're loaded. Negative thinkers who carry a lot of burden also feel like the last straw is a tough hump to get over—whether they live in the Middle East or the middle of nowhere.

All of this is why it's critical to watch your back as much as your front, especially since you can't see it. Making sure your back is covered, including your backside, gives you the best chance of finding a back door to exit, sneak out of, or run through. This may seem like backward thinking, but it's really forward thinking while back tracking.

Negativity Scale Checkpoint

Chapter 27: You Want Your Back against the Wall

1. You can look at my back and see I have one or more...

    a) Stress knots _____ (5 Points)
    b) People I need to get off it _____ (10 Points)
    c) Targets I'm trying to shake _____ (15 Points)
    d) Reasons to say, "Hey, back off!" _____ (20 Points)

2. The people watching my back lately are primarily...

    a) Backslappers _____ (5 Points)
    b) Backstabbers _____ (10 Points)
    c) Back-assward _____ (15 Points)
    d) On back order _____ (20 Points)

3. In the last 120 days, the number of last-straw-broken backs I suffered would have landed me in the Camel Spine Center for...

    a) One to three incidents _____ (5 Points)
    b) Four or five accidents _____ (10 Points)
    c) Six to ten emergencies _____ (15 Points)
    d) Countless intensive care visits _____ (20 Points)

4. If backs could talk, mine would love saying...

    a) "It's no skin off my back." _____ (5 Points)
    b) "Get off my back!" _____ (10 Points)
    c) "Let's go behind their back." _____ (15 Points)
    d) "Stop stabbing me in the back." _____ (20 Points)

5. **When my back is against the wall, I look right at the wall and...**

    a) Knock it down   _____ (5 Points)
    b) Read the handwriting   _____ (10 Points)
    c) Bang my head on it   _____ (15 Points)
    d) Find a hole and crawl in   _____ (20 Points)

Total Points, Chapter 27   _____

Lucky people take a round trip to hell and back.
Unlucky people go one way.

～

-28-

SHRINK YOUR CONFIDENCE WITHOUT A SHRINK

Positive thinkers stick to the pros. Negative thinkers identify with the cons. Words also have pros and cons. Oddly they can be negatively confusing but are never positively profusing.

Dictionary definition departments of publishing conglomerates, not proglomerates, defined confidence as a positive word. For some reason they bypassed "profidence" despite its popularity in Rhode Island. They got constipation right. No one would feel more confident doubled over with prostipation, which is why that most likely didn't pass either.

Even though confidence has a positive connotation instead of pronnotation, it also has far more in common with constipation. Both are things you don't want. How can you even have confidence in words when they don't cause constipation but are the root cause of verbal diarrhea? Let's continue since we can't protinue.

Confidence is nothing more than fuel for certainty, which is time and again uncertain. People who pump too much confidence through their body are instantly addicted. They feel almighty. Irresistible cravings for influence act like steroids on steroids to swell their psyches, growing them to massive proportions via high levels of stimulation to the striatum and prefrontal cortex. Once the transformation is complete, another gigantic jackass runs wild in the streets. No, this isn't a supernatural horror movie called *Psyches Gone Psycho*. For pessimists this reality gets no vote of confidence.

Everything from energy and egos to batteries and bottom lines requires a boost as time slowly drains them. Many fearless and determined leaders in the self-assurance field add confidence to the needs-a-boost-at-times list. Other experts who wrestle with false confidence support this position, even though they're somewhat hesitant or unsure.

Boosting anything, including confidence, is complicated. Energy boosts don't translate to confidence. A five-hour confidence shot supplement needs to be created to achieve this feat. The closest anyone has come are the makers of whiskey and tequila. Ego boosts go to people's heads. Boosting batteries is like trying to bring something back from the dead. Bottom-line boosts need to be done in confidence by having confidence, frequently with a staff that's lost confidence in a company desperately needing to reestablish confidence.

Many boxers are confident they're going to land a knockout punch, but they're often the ones who hit the canvas. Every politician is confident they're going to win their election, yet many more give a concession speech. Soon after, the people who voted quickly lose confidence. Groups of students are confident they'll get an A or a B, while plenty of others are sure they'll get a C, a D, or an F. Confidence is another positive thinker's vehicle that leaves you exposed to a crash.

There are different levels and perceptions of confidence. You can have every confidence. That's too many. You wouldn't be able to keep track of them all or even notice if you lost a few. There's always the option of placing your confidence in someone, although it might require an exorcism to get it back. Taking someone into your confidence is another option; however, it could get crowded depending on whether you've left more room for confidence. Trying to speak with confidence for those who lack it is like faking an accent. Betraying someone's confidence is risky, especially if you shared something they told you in strict confidence. Confidentially speaking, don't worry about having confidence.

The objective for negative thinkers is to maintain and sustain no confidence or be confidence neutral. Now confidence won't get in your way at all. You won't have too much or too little of it. There will never be a need to boost it, control it, or reel it in. Your only challenge is to not have the confidence you need to find happiness.

On the surface confidence is something people believe they have or perceive they're getting from someone or someplace else. Under the surface it's nothing more than a mind game.

There are two ways of analyzing this:

Pseudo-Psychological View—When a person convinces themself they have or need confidence, whether they do or they don't, it's no guarantee they will or they won't. Not many people have the confidence to accept this theory. They continue to build and boost their confidence, only to discover it's too difficult to keep their confidence, which is why they ultimately lose it.

Simple Layman's Terms—With even the highest level of confidence, things can still curdle in any situation. This is proven by bold cheeses, which get shredded every day after being built up as grate. Don't be cheese.

Negativity Scale Checkpoint

Chapter 28: Shrink Your Confidence without a Shrink

1. My confidence level this month is measuring…

    a) Sky high   _____ (5 Points)
    b) High enough   _____ (10 Points)
    c) The high end of low   _____ (15 Points)
    d) Low unless I get high   _____ (20 Points)

2. When I see someone doing something offensive in public, I have the confidence to…

    a) Ignore them   _____ (5 Points)
    b) Report them   _____ (10 Points)
    c) Encourage them   _____ (15 Points)
    d) Join them   _____ (20 Points)

3. For most of my life, the needle on my fuel gauge of confidence has pointed toward…

    a) "I'm full of it!"   _____ (5 Points)
    b) "I'm sure of it."   _____ (10 Points)
    c) "I'm iffy about it."   _____ (15 Points)
    d) "I'm not going near it."   _____ (20 Points)

4. The image my confidence makes me think of when I'm under pressure is a…

    a) Tough steak   _____ (5 Points)
    b) Crab cake   _____ (10 Points)
    c) Frozen block of ice   _____ (15 Points)
    d) Weeping willow   _____ (20 Points)

5. **The name of the board game that best captures my confidence is...**

   a) Battleship   _____ (5 Points)
   b) Boggle   _____ (10 Points)
   c) Trouble   _____ (15 Points)
   d) Sorry!   _____ (20 Points)

   Total Points, Chapter 28   _____

For what it's worth, there's a good chance it's worth nothing.

-29-

ASSUME THE NEGATIVE POSITION

You can assume everything on the menu at a restaurant looks yummy. It still doesn't mean the beef dish you order won't taste like Prime Cuts for Poochie. You could assume when you get someone's voicemail they're at the gym. But they could easily be at the dermatologist, getting a topical corticosteroid for psoriasis. You may assume someone is in love with you after three dates. In reality that's what the other two women or men he or she are seeing also think. Next thing you know, there are enough people involved to throw an orgy.

Trying to assume almost anything accurately is futile. Ask any couple who assumed they'd be together forever. Abounding numbers of them are now with other partners they assume they'll be with forever, as if they never heard of déjà relationship vu. See what countless people think now after assuming it was safe to be naked while they or someone in their home were connected to a Zoom meeting. Imagine how devastating it will be when the truth filters down to all the folks who still assume the earth is flat since it feels level when they walk, jog, and drive on it.

Unless you're a mind reader, assuming anything is a bad idea. It's like inserting your version of the story into the real story to create an altered story, which is a whole other story. When anyone says, "It's safe to assume blah, blah, blah..." take the position it's not safe to assume whatever they assumed. Assuming is always a crapshoot because what most people assume is usually unfounded crap that results in someone shooting themself in the foot or worse.

This clarifies why you hear the terms "false assumptions" and "wrong assumptions" far more than "right assumptions" and "true assumptions." A Google search [15] concurs:

"false assumptions"	=	653,000 results
"wrong assumptions"	=	285,000 results
"right assumptions"	=	43,000 results
"true assumptions"	=	20,800 results

Even "stupid assumptions" topped "right assumptions" and "true assumptions" combined, with 89,200 results.

How many times have you talked with someone on the phone you've never met and felt an unbelievable connection (with them, not the phone signal)? They've got an addicting voice, a stellar sense of humor, and you click in every way. You daydream about them, even if you have a significant other. The daydreams turn into fantasies. You envision making out with them at an exotic landmark or making a sex tape and getting over a million likes. When you finally meet, they have the face of a blobfish and appear to have undergone a personality displacement procedure.

Assumptions are nothing more than precarious predictions. Pessimists know this, which is why they never want to assume liability for anything. Even insurance companies that make a living assuming liabilities deny stacks of claims, while policyholders left in limbo are assuming they'll be paid.

Let's assume you assume someone is going to be on time for a lunch appointment. They assume you don't mind if they're fifteen minutes late. You assume they would have the courtesy to call and let you know they're running late. They assume you know they're coming and further assume you think being fifteen minutes late is no big deal. You assume they got into an accident and call local hospitals when they don't answer their phone. If they did go to the emergency room, they assume their insurance will pay a good portion of their bills. The insurance carrier assumes they're faking an injury and holds payment pending further investigation. It's a vicious cycle. Meanwhile you can assume none of this happened, but it could have, even if presumptively imagined. Either way no one correctly assumed lunch was doomed.

Only one kind of assumption is safe to make—a negative one. Always assume the worst. If the worst does happen, you assumed right and can take solace in seeing it coming. If you assumed wrong, and less than the worst happens, you got lucky and can take satisfaction in knowing it could have been worse. It's a win-win for the negative team because they assumed the worst or the least of the worst was coming. On the other hand, if you assume something positive and it turns out negative, you feel the full force of the unexpected outcome, which you never saw coming.

In conclusion when you talk to someone on the phone for the first time, assume they'll remind you of a personality-challenged blobfish in person. When you have insurance claims, assume they won't pay without a fight. Finally, if you schedule a lunch appointment, assume whomever you're meeting may be late or stop to consult ER doctors on the way.

You'll be happier when your negative assumptions turn out to be more accurate and acceptable—whether they're correct or incorrect.

Negativity Scale Checkpoint

Chapter 29: Assume the Negative Position

1. **When I meet someone, they probably assume I'm...**

   a) Out of the ordinary   _____ (5 Points)
   b) Out of their league   _____ (10 Points)
   c) Out of my mind   _____ (15 Points)
   d) Out on bail   _____ (20 Points)

2. **When I leave a message for a close friend and don't hear back that day, I assume they're...**

   a) Busy   _____ (5 Points)
   b) Flaky   _____ (10 Points)
   c) Mad at me   _____ (15 Points)
   d) In a ditch, kidnapped, or worse   _____ (20 Points)

3. **My assumptions have about as much chance of coming true as they do of me...**

   a) Having a birthday this year   _____ (5 Points)
   b) Getting a strange look from a stranger   _____ (10 Points)
   c) Not laughing when someone walks into a sliding glass door   _____ (15 Points)
   d) Sweeping an ocean floor   _____ (20 Points)

4. **People I work with for the first time assume I'm...**

   a) Ingeniously intelligent   _____ (5 Points)
   b) Infinitely inspiring   _____ (10 Points)
   c) Ignorantly inept   _____ (15 Points)
   d) Infuriatingly insane   _____ (20 Points)

5. **If the Assumption Association of America analyzed the way I assume, they would assume...**

   a) It is logically based on something I presume _____ (5 Points)
   b) It may or may not lead to feelings of gloom _____ (10 Points)
   c) It has a good chance of making me fume _____ (15 Points)
   d) It means at any moment something could go boom _____ (20 Points)

   Total Points, Chapter 29 _____

Beware of people who talk behind
your back in front of your face.

~

-30-

SURVIVING IN THE SCREW YOUNIVERSE

It's only a matter of time before you'll be a statistic of YESS—you're eventually screwed syndrome. How often you'll be screwed is unknown; however, your odds increase astronomically whenever you interact with any human or microbiological entity.

The mentality of the universe has shifted to "me," which means "you" are vulnerable. In a telling sign of how screwy things are, whispers are circulating about lawyers representing Scooby-Doo issuing a cease-and-desist letter to stop a new rapper from using the name Screw-Yoo-Too-Bee-Doo.

Three laws rule the screw youniverse. The first is Murphy's law—whatever can go wrong will go wrong. [16] Optimists take this as inspiration to uncover what could go wrong before it goes wrong, to prevent it from going wrong. They obviously think three wrongs make a right, but they're wrong. When plans go awry, everyone is screwed. Negative thinkers interpret the law differently. They accept there is little chance of anything going right. Hence they strengthen their screwmunity and develop a resistance to microwronganisms.

Walking around your home seems safe. Yet at some point, you're going to stub your toe on a piece of possessed furniture that rolled into your path even though it's not on wheels. Chances are no one will be there to see you writhing around in pain on the floor like shrimp shimmying on a sizzling-hot hibachi grill. Why does this happen, you wonder? For shrimp it's because they're delicious. For you toe-stubbing serves as a reminder you're always one step away from an unexpected negative experience.

The law of averages is the second law. It's based on the idea that over time you can expect the probability of specific outcomes to happen at a frequency determined by how often it has already happened. You may need an above-average attorney to further explain this law to you.

Here's how an attorney-not-at-law might sum it up: if you're at a casino roulette wheel, and eight spins in a row land on black, you may feel red is due. You bet red thinking the law of averages is on your side since it's statistically improbable for the ball to land on black every time until the apocalypse. When the ninth black in a row hits, you're screwed and a little poorer. If you're on a multi-year losing streak, it doesn't mean you're due for a win. What it may signify is you should stay away from the roulette table and try online bingo.

Regardless of statistical data, pessimists believe the law of averages relies too much on complicated math. It's like trying to solve those problems they give you in school: Natasha has six cans of soup that weigh 14.5 ounces each. Boris has nine cobs of corn, each weighing an average of 1.37 pounds. Natasha trades Boris three of her cans for two of his cobs. How much weight will Natasha put on if she eats two cobs and three bowls of soups with three ounces of 0.6-inch-in-diameter oyster crackers? Without the help of representatives from H&R Block and Weight Watchers, the law of averages isn't on the side of most students, scholars, or CFOs getting it right.

A negative person who keeps getting hit by cars knows to stay away from main roads, side streets, parking lots, and car transport trucks. A positive person might believe the law of averages predicts the typical person doesn't get hit by cars in great numbers over a lifetime. They may think they've been hit by more than their share of vehicles already, or they won't get hit at all, so the odds are in their favor. This may explain why uncounted numbers of positive-thinking pedestrians end up in a crosswalk with their face pressed against a car's front axle. The most important statistic to remember about the law of averages is if you've been screwed before you're going to get screwed again.

Law number three is Larry's law of the screw youniverse: when you expect to be screwed, it's harder for someone to nail you. In a screwed-up world where lunacy is the new normal, it's hard not to encounter some screwball wherever you go. This increases your exposure to loonies with a screw loose looking to put the screws to you or screw you over. Negative thinking prepares and protects you from whoever or whatever that is by helping you keep your head screwed on right.

Survival of the fittest has evolved into survival of the screwiest. Being in shape, owning a gym membership, or participating in extreme workouts isn't enough to survive each day. You need to be fit for society too. The screwiest are also surviving by replicating like clones who duplicate and emulate each other's eccentric behaviors like mirror images, faster than reproductions coming out of a copy machine. Based on this scenario, history will repeat itself, and future generations will also be screwed.

Accepting you will be screwed regularly will help you develop the negative defenses necessary to survive in the screw youniverse. Once you do you'll have the ability to find happiness while getting screwed over and over again.

Negativity Scale Checkpoint

Chapter 30: Surviving in the Screw Youniverse

1. **In the screw youniverse…**

   a) I don't get screwed much　　　_____ (5 Points)
   b) I get screwed often enough　　_____ (10 Points)
   c) I screw others more than
      they screw me　　　　　　　　_____ (15 Points)
   d) All I can say is screw this
      question and screw you!　　　_____ (20 Points)

2. **Based on real-life screw youniverse experiences, the movie sequel most appropriate for me to star in is…**

   a) *The Taming of the Screw*　　_____ (5 Points)
   b) *Mo' Better Screws*　　　　　 _____ (10 Points)
   c) *More Than One Screw
      over the Cuckoo's Nest*　　　 _____ (15 Points)
   d) *The Man/Woman Who
      Screws Too Much*　　　　　　 _____ (20 Points)

3. **When screwing someone hypothetically or in real life, my style is to…**

   a) Turn the screw quickly　　　　_____ (5 Points)
   b) Turn the screw slowly　　　　 _____ (10 Points)
   c) Bang the screw in with a hammer　_____ (15 Points)
   d) Drive the screw in with an
      electric screwdriver　　　　　_____ (20 Points)

4. My survival instincts are linked to ...

   a) Survival of the sexiest   _____ (5 Points)
   b) Survival of the profoundest   _____ (10 Points)
   c) Survival of the naughtiest   _____ (15 Points)
   d) Survival of the who gives a bleepest _____ (20 Points)

5. When push comes to shove in this dog-eat-dog world, my defense reflex is to...

   a) Lick   _____ (5 Points)
   b) Bark   _____ (10 Points)
   c) Growl   _____ (15 Points)
   d) Bite   _____ (20 Points)

Total Points, Chapter 30   _____

Too often you'll find that what matters doesn't matter at all.

-31-

THE PROBLEM WITH PROBLEMS

You can learn a lot about problems from landscapers. They know how to find the root of something, weed it out, and control how big it grows. If all else fails, they're also experts on the effects of smoking grass.

Before public records were kept, it is suspected landscapers in the early 1900s initiated the practice of smoking weed to better handle their problems. This created more problems ranging from respiratory ailments to poisonings as they failed to take into consideration that what they were smoking was bathed in weed killer. Once they started toking premium weed without herbicides, they cared a lot less about their problems. One unintended consequence is this method of solving problems put the munchies industry on the map. This led to weight and teeth problems. Soon problems gave birth to other problems, which explains the term problem child.

Positive people always exclaim, "No problem!" This phrase lost its meaning when it became the go-to replacement for "You're welcome."

"Thank you for doing that."

"No problem!"

If someone asks you to do something, why clarify that it's not a problem if it isn't a problem? It's kind of like eating a meal and declaring, "No indigestion!" Would you want to hear an airplane pilot announce right after landing, "No crash!"? How about someone who performs circumcisions wrapping up and declaring for all to hear, "No shaky hands!"?

Another misused positive response you can't trust is "I have no problem with that." Let's say an unhappily married man tells a friend he has to take his wife's car to the repair shop to have her worn brakes replaced. The friend says, "I watched a video on brake repairs and fixed my wife's car. Would you like me to give it a shot?"

The guy in the lousy marriage replies, "I have no problem with that. Give me a few hours to call my agent and increase my wife's life insurance benefit." There is no standard for determining what people have a problem with, which is an odd problem since there is a substandard.

If you can't deal with problems of any kind, one approach is to stick with "That's your problem" or "That's not my problem." Don't accept or acknowledge any problem whatsoever. You can't stress over or solve a problem you don't have. There's no more effective way to stay problem free than to invalidate every problem by categorizing it as a problem that's not for you.

The biggest problem with problems for most earthlings is they're problematic. True negative thinkers develop an uncanny ability to see problems even before they appear. They'll think, "That's the problem," or, "What's your problem?" or, "One problem..."

You don't have to be a psychic or a psychoneurotic to predict problems. You do need to be aware there are problems around every corner, yet you can't avoid them by always walking straight and never turning.

Here's how to attack problems before they attack you:

Problem Predicament Pointers

Treat Problems like a Pizza Pie—The more people who share a problem, the more who can be responsible for whatever goes wrong. Cut the problem into slices and serve it with your favorite negative toppings.

Overthink Every Single Problem—Once a problem enters your brain, it disperses, bombarding your consciousness, subconscious, unconsciousness, and semiconsciousness. Success here is difficult for anyone who has no consciousness. Results vary between someone's unconscious mind and the minds of individuals who have been knocked out cold.

Sleep on Your Problems—It may be uncomfortable to sleep on anything other than a bed and a pillow, but add your problems to that list for two reasons:

1. The characters in your dreams are often smarter than the ones you know in real life and could help solve them.
2. Well-rested people are better at tackling tough problems after dreaming about being superheroes, rock stars, and love gods or goddesses.

Determine If the Problem Passes the Shit Test—To see whether a problem is worth solving, it should generate at least one "yes" answer to the following questions:

> Do I give a shit?
> Will anyone else give a shit?
> Is this a shitstorm waiting to happen?
> Will doing this land me on anyone's shit list?
> Should I prepare for a trip up shit creek?
> Am I avoiding this because I'm a chickenshit?
> Will anyone beat the shit out of me?

Negativity Scale Checkpoint

Chapter 31: The Problem with Problems

1. **My approach to handling problems is to…**

   a) Use logic and reasoning _____ (5 Points)
   b) Get—or pay—someone else
   to solve it _____ (10 Points)
   c) Stuff my face with food _____ (15 Points)
   d) Change my name, address,
   and/or phone number _____ (20 Points)

2. **I believe for every problem there is…**

   a) A way to make it go away _____ (5 Points)
   b) A silver or cubic zirconia lining _____ (10 Points)
   c) A load of BS to go with it _____ (15 Points)
   d) A fun or naughty distraction
   to take my mind off it _____ (20 Points)

3. **My personal attitude regarding problems is…**

   a) "What problem?" _____ (5 Points)
   b) "It's a minor setback." _____ (10 Points)
   c) "My problems are yours too." _____ (15 Points)
   d) "This isn't going to end well." _____ (20 Points)

4. **The problems I have are mostly caused by…**

   a) Things that breathe _____ (5 Points)
   b) Things that don't breathe _____ (10 Points)
   c) Things that breathe and don't breathe _____ (15 Points)
   d) Me when I breathe _____ (20 Points)

5. At this exact moment I have...

    a) Between zero and five problems   _____ (5 Points)
    b) About six to ten problems   _____ (10 Points)
    c) Too many problems to count   _____ (15 Points)
    d) So many problems it's a miracle I'm not in a room with padded walls   _____ (20 Points)

Total Points, Chapter 31   _____

If wisdom teeth are so smart,
why do they get pulled?

-32-

BE AN IMPERFECTIONIST

An off-the-record report that was allegedly leaked from the National Institute of Notoriously Nitpicking Yammerers (NINNY) insinuates several remarkable observations. Its analysis pinpoints how perfectionists are self-centered fanatics who struggle with self-inflicted insanity, obtuse obsessiveness, and inclinations involving intense isolation. It further suggests these are feelings and behaviors perfectionists relish as much as hot dog lovers relish their relish. This suspiciously signifies that the need for individuals to be or appear perfect is an illusion or a delusion, which can lead to seclusion. On top of that, wiener-eating perfectionists may also suffer from hot dog heartburn, relish reflux, and foot-long flatulence.

An uncorroborated verbal statement from an obscure organization called Don't Expect Flawless Execution Can Transpire (DEFECT) tells another side of the story. DEFECT's research reveals being an imperfectionist isn't even on the radar for the lion's share of human beings. When asked why, a spokeswoman replied, "Because 'imperfectionist' isn't a series of letters that form a real word yet." She added that their studies of imperfectionotics specifically alludes in the abstract a steady rise in imperfectionism, which provides direct and indirect paths to satisfaction that are far from perfect.

Dissecting everything in pursuit of perfection is a losing proposition. Picking things apart to evaluate all the negative aspects—without attempting to rectify or perfectivize them—is where negative mindsets should be going. This is also an imperfect statement since "perfectivize" isn't a word either. That's how groundbreaking this thinking is—there are few words to describe it. In fact brand new clinical trials to study the effects of imperfectionism on unbiased minds are currently in the infant stage. Conclusive findings aren't expected to be available until the subjects are able to talk.

Negative thinkers learn to reject any form of perfection. Nothing is perfectly acceptable when you refuse to accept perfection. Every day plenty of once-perfect matches head for Splitsville. Jails are full of perfectionists who believed they were committing the perfect crime. It's impossible to live in perfect harmony unless you're a member of Crosby, Stills, Nash, and sometimes Young or You. Perfect strangers? It's absurd to think strangers are any more perfect than folks in the flesh you already know. You can believe something is a perfect fit, but how could it be if you don't have a perfect body?

An author may try to write every sentence perfectly. This illustrates why it took over a half century to write this book, while it would have taken a perfectionist closer to a century. Lots of authors never get past chapter one, as they rewrite it over and over. Scores of writers intentionally keep their stories short. The advantage is that there are fewer words to perfect in telling their stories. One brilliant, best-selling short story author did this hundreds of times. Even his publisher often said in disbelief, "Oh, Henry."

Buyers of greeting cards fall into the perfection trap too. Huge numbers of sentiment senders spend hours, even days, trying to write an impeccable emotional message. After struggling they frequently end up purchasing another card since the one they added all the inkblots and crossed out words to looks like a Rorschach test. Imperfectionists find cards containing a huge number of prewritten words—so there's less room to fit in anything original—or settle for a few select words of choice and write them ultra-big to take up more space.

Another solution is scribbling a bunch of illegible words that look like they're written in a code hackers who infiltrate banks, government agencies, and big businesses couldn't crack. Then it doesn't matter what you write because no one can read it anyway. It's still appreciated by the recipient.

If you live with someone special and want to conserve words and money, go into the drawer where they saved all the previous cards you gave them. Add a new date under the original date and give it back to them. It's like recycling a preapproved message.

One life is too short for perfection. The time it takes to make something perfect calls for being reincarnated repeatedly. By trying to do everything at home, work, and in relationships to perfection, you'll drive everyone you encounter nuts, including yourself. It also does not mean you'll get thanked, paid, or laid any more than if you had done it imperfectly.

Being a perfectionist is like going into a heavyweight fight with yourself, only there's a good possibility you might get knocked out in every round. Analyzing the imperfections of situations opens your eyes to where the punches you're about to absorb are coming from. You're then empowered to counterpunch by jabbing away at the most preferrable of the unpreferable options. It's not healthy to think, "I'm going to get it right even if it kills me." Cemeteries are filled with people who died trying.

All citizens of civilized and uncivilized societies should accept that nothing and no one is perfect. Even the word "perfect" isn't perfect. It describes something that only exists in theory. Optimists still express, "In a perfect world…" when in reality, it's more logical to state, "In an imperfect world…"

This makes everything and everyone perfectly imperfect.

Negativity Scale Checkpoint

Chapter 32: Be an Imperfectionist

1. In my mind, "practice makes perfect" can also be translated to mean...

    a) "I'll get this right!" _____ (5 Points)
    b) "Close enough." _____ (10 Points)
    c) "When wax stops building up in my ears." _____ (15 Points)
    d) "No #@%&!* way!" _____ (20 Points)

2. If a psychologist engaged me in sound association with the word perfection, my response would be...

    a) "Yeeeeaah!" _____ (5 Points)
    b) "Bah" _____ (10 Points)
    c) "Gah" _____ (15 Points)
    d) "Waah!" _____ (20 Points)

3. The closest I've ever come to perfection is...

    a) Millimeters _____ (5 Points)
    b) Horse lengths _____ (10 Points)
    c) Nautical miles _____ (15 Points)
    d) Light-years _____ (20 Points)

4. My strategy when determining how perfect something needs to be is...

    a) Leave no room for error _____ (5 Points)
    b) Leave little room for error _____ (10 Points)
    c) Leave lots of room for error _____ (15 Points)
    d) Leave the room entirely _____ (20 Points)

5. **When I look back on my life, many things weren't perfect because I did them...**

   a) Without reason   _____ (5 Points)
   b) Without permission   _____ (10 Points)
   c) Without warning   _____ (15 Points)
   d) Without knowing jack   _____ (20 Points)

Total Points, Chapter 32   _____

Happiness may come from within,
but unhappiness comes from without.

-33-

MIST UNDERSTANDINGS

It is possible to be happily negative. The secret is in how you channel your negativity. For starters avoid confusing pessimists with these other kinds of mists:

> **Pissimists:** Perpetually angry soreheads whose jaws are clenched tighter than the two butt cheeks of a lactose-intolerant sufferer who ate a milk product and is three minutes away from the closest bathroom.

> **Contradictimists:** They swing back and forth from pro to con faster than a pair of eyeballs watching a replay of the Chinese table tennis championships in fast-forward.

> **Dismalimists:** Gloomy, dreary people who make DMV employees look like they're cheery and moving fast.

> **Earplugimists:** These folks march to the beat of a different eardrum. It doesn't matter what you say; they will never hear you.

> **Difficultimists:** So impossible to please, they make you wish you had a voodoo doll of them to stick with pins.

> **Woodpeckerimists:** Every conversation with these birdbrains makes you feel like you're a tree trunk being pecked apart as they hammer home pointless points.

> **Moodimists:** Mood rings even short-circuit on these temperamental swingers. Be in no mood for them.

> **Gasbagimists:** The only enjoyment they get is hearing the sound of their own tongues flapping around in the hot air blowing out of their mouths.

> **Deceiverimists:** Everything might be negative to them, but don't be fooled. They can mislead a horse to water and not only make it drink, they'll convince it to gargle.

> **Bullshitimists:** Anything they say, positive or negative, will burn your nose hairs.

Developing a negative mindset doesn't mean you need to support it with undesirable character traits. You can find fault with something without being an off-putting sourpuss or going junkyard-dog, au-contraire aggressive. How you deliver your negativity is crucial. There's a big difference between a woman saying after a bad date, "What an ass," and a donkey breeder saying it during mating season. If the donkey breeder said it like the upset woman, and the upset woman said it like the donkey breeder, it would make the same point but in a different tone.

There is one more kind of mist to consider—the optimist. Medical experts preach that there is a link between better health and being optimistic. According to one study involving thousands of people over thirty years, optimists live as much as 15 percent longer than pessimists. [17] Even still, regardless of optimistic or pessimistic persuasion, the vast majority of the general public do look happy and upbeat in their obituary photos.

The study's findings make the mind wander. Did the focus group include blue collar, white collar, collarless, and dog-collar workers? Or were they a mix of trust fund beneficiaries, celebrities who've completed rehab, and athletes brought up on charges within the last five years?

Compared to optimists who live up to 15 percent longer, did they also look into whether participants who are 50 percent optimists and 50 percent pessimists live up to 7.5 percent longer?

There's another side to the story too. Other findings reveal how being pessimistic may be surprisingly beneficial for performance, confidence, and health. The research explores "defensive pessimism," where pessimism and negative thinking can be used as positive psychology, leading to achieving goals and personal growth. [18] In this case defensive pessimism goes much deeper than what sports teams who keep getting blown out every game are feeling. It gets further complicated when the offensive unit turns on the defense in every way except sexually.

As you become more proficient in negative thinking, stay defensive. Not being defensive has been tested unsuccessfully by inept militaries, burned-out attorneys, and hikers on trails in the wilderness who didn't bring bear spray.

There are obnoxious optimists, inspiring pessimists, and every other kind of positive or negative personality combination in between. Customize negativity to your personal image, behavior, and lifestyle. If you're not happy with your own qualities, consider a multi-year subscription to the Self-Help Book of the Month Club for additional support. As you progress it will get easier to clear up mist understandings.

Negativity Scale Checkpoint

Chapter 33: Mist Understandings

1. As far as the optimist versus pessimist tug-of-war goes, I'm tugging toward...

    a) Happy optimist _____ (5 Points)
    b) Seasonal hoper _____ (10 Points)
    c) Bah-humbug cynic _____ (15 Points)
    d) Merry pessimist _____ (20 Points)

2. In my mind it's no secret that optimists...

    a) Have the right attitude _____ (5 Points)
    b) Brainwash themselves _____ (10 Points)
    c) Are super gullible _____ (15 Points)
    d) Nauseate me _____ (20 Points)

3. If you followed me around for the last three months, you would have seen hanging over my head...

    a) A halo _____ (5 Points)
    b) A light bulb _____ (10 Points)
    c) One big, black cloud _____ (15 Points)
    d) The Sword of Damocles _____ (20 Points)

4. It's hard for me to grasp why pessimists are so...

    a) Mistaken _____ (5 Points)
    b) Misguided _____ (10 Points)
    c) Misunderstood _____ (15 Points)
    d) Mistreated _____ (20 Points)

5. If an optimist and a pessimist were locked in a steel cage for twenty-four hours, it would end with the...

    a) Match declared a draw   _____ (5 Points)
    b) Pessimist crying uncle   _____ (10 Points)
    c) Optimist begging for mercy   _____ (15 Points)
    d) Optimist, pessimist, referee, and audience in tears   _____ (20 Points)

Total Points, Chapter 33   _____

Curiosity didn't kill the cat. Being optimistic it could cross the street without getting hit by a car or truck did.

-34-

PLAY ALL THE NEGATIVE ANGLES

We're conditioned from the time we open our eyes to see things right side up. This provides a limited view of life, which is often upside down. One group that appreciates the upside-down perspective are those capable of doing a handstand. A short-lived organization called Get Off Your Feet once tried to lead an upside-down movement and open the public's eyes by going mainstream with walking handstands. Aside from a bunch of broken hips, the biggest complaint was participants being unable to get used to wearing shoes on their hands and gloves on their feet. Right side up still stands in most countries, and so do the limitations that come with it.

Negative thinkers analyze every situation from all sides. Packages understand this concept better than humans. It doesn't matter if they're labeled "this side up," they still get where they're going any side up. Try shipping yourself somewhere and observe the world from a viewpoint you've never seen. Don't forget to put a few holes in the box for a better view and air. There's a built-in, added perk if you've never traveled first class before.

Optimists don't think of positivity having a downside, only an upside. Pessimists know there's an upside to negativity. By exposing as many negative angles as possible, expected and unexpected blows are identified ahead of time. As the captain of the Viking ship *Norse to the Grindstone* famously shouted to his oarsmen, "This boat will not sink if you woe, woe, woe."

You don't need a master's degree in geometry to grasp the essence of negative angles. You'll always get a different perspective considering things downside up. It's similar to bottoms up without the drinks. Upside up and downside down are extreme views and always worth a look when you're experiencing ups and downs. Side angles are fascinating, depending on what side you're on.

There are situations involving right angles that can leave you boxed into a corner. Watch out for anyone who comes at you from the opposite side of a right angle. They're nothing more than a hypotenuisance. Scenarios involving acute angles may not be so cute. When they're hiding something unattractive, it's harder to align interests. Straight angles are deceptive. One minute you're moving forward, the next you're doing a complete 180. When under pressure, reflex angles need to be carefully inspected. They're famous for eliciting knee-jerk reactions without putting much thought into it. When you're looking at a full angle, you'll have to double check to verify it's actually full versus half full or half empty. On occasion you'll find yourself caught in an obtuse angle. These are the most difficult angles since they don't have a point.

Evaluating negative angles keeps all your options in view. You'll be less likely to go off on a tangent. It protects you from unscrupulous people with ulterior motives playing an angle. Beware of them; they're only out for themselves. Those kinds of manipulators are multiplying faster than organisms reproducing by binary fission on public toilets. Never bend over backward or forward for them.

The formula for finding negative angle gratification (NAG) is: The sum of the sides is directly related to the ratio of success or failure, determined by the combined chosen angles and powered by a negative mindset.

Sum of Combined Sides (/+\+|+|+ −)
[Determined by Chosen Angles]
_____
Ratio of Success (Sunny Side) = Bright Sum
or Failure (Dark Side) = Dim Sum

Observing the world solely from positive angles will eventually yield unexpected negative results. Analyzing the full array of negative angles allows you to see the many sides of a situation, including conversations, competitions, relationships, and eyewitness accounts that are all one sided.

Life is meant to be looked at from different angles. If everyone analyzed things from the same point of view, it would mean humans raised by *Homo sapiens* would see, do, and think no differently than people raised by wolves or the internet.

Negativity Scale Checkpoint

Chapter 34: Play All the Negative Angles

1. I have more trouble playing angles on…

   a) Sides and straightaways   _____ (5 Points)
   b) Corners and turns   _____ (10 Points)
   c) Ups and downs   _____ (15 Points)
   d) Ups, downs, corners, turns, sides, and straightaways   _____ (20 Points)

2. When I analyze things, the focus of my mind is on…

   a) Only positive angles   _____ (5 Points)
   b) All positive and negative angles   _____ (10 Points)
   c) Isolating negative angles   _____ (15 Points)
   d) Why I suffer from a fear of angles   _____ (20 Points)

3. If the Angle Association of the Americas, Eurasia, and Antarctica named an angle for me, they'd call it the…

   a) Everything-goes-right angle   _____ (5 Points)
   b) Play-it-straight angle   _____ (10 Points)
   c) Acid-reflex angle   _____ (15 Points)
   d) Let-me-dangle-while-I-tangle-and-mangle angle   _____ (20 Points)

4. After considering all the angles, I'm more drawn to…

   a) Right side up   _____ (5 Points)
   b) Upside down   _____ (10 Points)
   c) Inside out   _____ (15 Points)
   d) Lying flat with my eyes closed   _____ (20 Points)

5. **I wish I had a guardian angle to…**

   a) Make sure my angles measure up _____ (5 Points)
   b) Protect me from angles with
      sharp edges _____ (10 Points)
   c) Help me stop playing so many
      losing angles _____ (15 Points)
   d) Put an end to me being
      attacked from every angle _____ (20 Points)

   Total Points, Chapter 34 _____

If nothing lasts forever, even forever won't last.

~

-35-

LOOK ON THE BLAH SIDE

Optimists who look on the bright side need to get their positive-peering peepers checked. It's all an illusion—like when people who don't look good in photos think they look good in mirrors, when in fact, they only look good in pitch-black darkness. Positive thinkers believe beauty is in the eye of the beholder. Negative theorists think the only thing their eyes behold are cataracts.

Looking on the bright side is another hopeful false promise. It's the same flawed logic as "the grass is always greener on the other side." Maybe it is if they're using a high-grade fertilizer, but that doesn't count. It's not brighter or greener there in terms of happiness. If it looks, smells, and tastes like grass, it is grass. Next time you think the grass is greener someplace else, graze on it. Then graze the grass on the side you started. It's just grass any way you cut it. Get off the grass fixation and stop judging how green it is. If you're still feeling sheepish after that, when you go to sleep try counting blahs instead of baas.

Positive thinkers focus on happier times when things are bleak. This doesn't help anyone climb out of a current hole in which they are feeling upset, disrespected, unappreciated, or disheartened. Holes are also much easier to get into than out of, which is baffling since they have the same exit, entrance, and radius all around. While optimists are digging holes for themselves from dashed hopes, pessimists are shooting holes through everything to see through them. Holes are not happy areas unless you have an ace in one. All other holes, with the possible exception of a watering hole, you need like a hole in the head. Let's not even touch a——holes.

If you've found true happiness, it's not because you've been looking on the bright side. Perhaps you're easy to please. It's a numbers game, and the odds are stacked against you. The have-nots outcount the haves. The luckless outnumber the fortunate. The stupid outbreed the smart. The disgusting outgross the disgusted. The outsitting outwait the outstanding. If there is a bright side, it's not always easy to see.

We can gain valuable knowledge from birds who fly south for the winter, especially snowbirds. When the weather turns cold, they go south in search of warmth, but their problems follow them. Yet when situations go south, most individuals prefer to chill. From every direction, regardless of temperature, the common denominator is south. One adjustment you can make is to convince yourself whatever direction you're facing is north. It is accepted, albeit not widely, that this might cut down on problems by preventing things from going south. Think of it as the equivalent of quandary border control.

There are various levels of happiness and unhappiness—from unhappy and not-too happy to pretty happy and hyper happy to unhappy as the day is long and happy as a pig in shit. Negative thinkers are happy to get through the day with the least amount of terrible stuff happening.

Being happy can be misleading. When someone says, "Happy to see you," are they telling the truth? At least with "unhappy to see you," it's obvious how they feel and where you stand. Oodles of people say they're as happy as a clam, but it's doubtful they've been to a clam bake. Have you seen a happy clam? Don't even get into being happy as a lark. This whole line of thinking is a lark. Happiness is so deceptive; even during happy hour, which extends well past an hour, bars have to ply you with free appetizers and discounted alcoholic drinks to keep you happy. Isn't it strange that you can always toast happiness, but you can't always trust it?

Looking on the bright side of adversity is absurd. Let's say a friend comes to you and confides she got trichomoniasis from a guy she met on a blind date. What's the bright side—she finally had sex after six years, or it's not as bad as crabs? A close relative loses his job. What's the bright side—more time to golf and binge watch shows, or great news—Uncle

Angus is eligible for food stamps!? Your home gets flooded when a pipe bursts. What's the bright side—you've got a terrific plumber, or you've always wanted an indoor pool?

The reality is there is no bright side to trichomoniasis, getting fired, or your home getting flooded. This is why it's better to keep things real and look on the blah side. Then if a friend reveals she has trichomoniasis you can say, "How terrible," while thinking to yourself, "She's wearing shorts; I hope she doesn't hug me." Or if a relative loses his job you can say, "I'm so sorry," while secretly muttering, "He never sends so much as a birthday card; I hope he doesn't ask for a loan." Or when your home floods, you can say, "What a mess," followed by, "Honey, we need to go shopping for a kayak and snorkels!"

How long can you keep seeing the positive side of things without feeling like you're trying to fool yourself? Life will keep throwing crap at you, and it's not distributed evenly or fairly. As Admiral Bird said, looking up to the sky on many occasions, "If a bird craps on you, it's a reminder that the shit's the limit."

Looking at the blah side keeps your blahs in check. There are no positive false hopes, wishful thoughts, or prayers involved. At the beginning of the world, everything was new. Hardly anything went wrong. You could only see a bright side. Now the world is weighed down in problems. When you can't see the bright side, things may look brighter on the blah side.

Negativity Scale Checkpoint

Chapter 35: Look on the Blah Side

1. During the past year, the light bulb illuminating the bright side of my life has been a...

    a) One hundred-to-one-hundred-fifty-watt bulb _____ (5 Points)
    b) Sixty-to-seventy-five-watt bulb _____ (10 Points)
    c) Twenty-five-to-forty-watt bulb _____ (15 Points)
    d) Bulb that burned out long ago _____ (20 Points)

2. If I were a superhero, and things worked out the way they usually do for me, the vast majority of victims I save would be somewhere between...

    a) Grateful and indebted _____ (5 Points)
    b) Frustrated and agitated _____ (10 Points)
    c) Shocked and appalled _____ (15 Points)
    d) Terror stricken and pushing up daisies _____ (20 Points)

3. As far as the unknown goes, my feelings would best be captured on a bumper sticker that read...

    a) Fearless Evermore _____ (5 Points)
    b) Cool. Calm. Confused. _____ (10 Points)
    c) Better Off Blindfolded _____ (15 Points)
    d) Not Ready. Not Willing. Not Able. _____ (20 Points)

4. **My philosophy regarding news affecting my life is...**

    a) Good news is great news   _____ (5 Points)
    b) No news is bad news   _____ (10 Points)
    c) Bad news is the only news   _____ (15 Points)
    d) Skip the news; give me weather and sports   _____ (20 Points)

5. **Based on how excited I am about my future, the category I would pick first on *Jeopardy!* is...**

    a) Heigh-Ho, Heigh-Ho, It's off to What's Next I Go   _____ (5 Points)
    b) The Skittish Are Coming! The Skittish Are Coming!   _____ (10 Points)
    c) Prepare for a Rough Landing   _____ (15 Points)
    d) Run Away! Run Away!   _____ (20 Points)

Total Points, Chapter 35   _____

You'll be amazed by how far you can go
by first seeing how far you can't go.

-36-

THE BITTER END

Of all the life-changing obstacles we face, death is by far the deadliest. You can't beat it, cheat it, or defeat it. From the moment you are born, every second moves you one day closer to the bitter end. Even its top representative—the grim reaper—wears a dark, hooded, black robe, carries a scythe, and is scary as hell when he comes to collect some poor soul's soul. It's not exactly a welcoming sign, especially if you're headed for heaven. Why isn't there a grin keeper to greet us with a smile instead of a terrifying dude who's ready to reap us like a harvest crop? That alone proves death is not meant to be a positive experience.

Optimists put a positive spin on eternal rest. It does sound relaxing. They'll tell you you're going to the great beyond. Perhaps they think it's great because everyone goes there, they're never fully booked, and no one ever comes home. They'll say whoever passed has gone to a better place. How do they know it's better? No one ever returned with photos or a souvenir "I survived the great beyond" T-shirt. This makes it difficult to verify what it's like there or to post a titillating review on Tripadvisor confirming it is a definite, don't-miss-it bucket-list destination.

Most living people never think about dying when they're young. As they get older, they go out of their way to try not to think about it. Unless you work at a funeral home, death generally isn't on the top two hundred list of conversation starters for dinner parties. Everyone knows they're going to die, yet they learn to live with it. If your soul does live on, your body is still celestial or hellestial toast. Even if someone has a bone to pick with you, it won't matter one bit once you're a skeleton. Using death as a motivator while you're living makes complete sense since relying on life as a catalyst after you're dead isn't nearly as uplifting.

As a society we've come to believe death is untimely. Don't believe it. There is no such thing as an untimely death. When anyone dies and a doctor is around, the first thing he or she announces is, "Time of death: whatever o'clock." This makes all deaths timely. When your clock has run out, it's game over. Even if you were born before your time, you don't get extra time. Take the story of Grandma Trixie. At her funeral shocked mourners could hear a voice from within the coffin six feet under. It was eleven o'clock. Her talking watch reminded everyone it was clearly past her time.

Earth was formed about 4.5 billion years ago. There was a long waiting list to get here, but the planet did fine without humans for billions of years. It'll also keep going long after your demise. According to NASA, the universe consists of 68 percent dark energy and 27 percent dark matter. [19] There doesn't appear to be a statistic that factors in all the people on earth who appear to be in the dark. This translates to 95 percent of the universe being made up of dark forces. Even with all the efforts of light bulb manufacturers, including the switch to LED, nothing has made the future of the universe's composition any less dark.

The remaining 5 percent consists of energy and normal matter—visible things like light, x-rays, the sun, comets, galaxies, and rhinoceroses. [19] The real question is: Why does any of this matter? That's the point. The world is way bigger than you are. Atlas once held the sky on his shoulders as a punishment from Zeus. He went home with a herniated disc, cervical radiculopathy, and poor posture. For his trouble they named a beautiful collection of maps in his name.

In a universe fueled by dark matter and dark energy, where everything ends in death for whatever lives, it's worth questioning whether positive thinking should rule. If you haven't found happiness through positive thinking, perhaps its power has worn off in an increasingly not-so-positive dark world. The alternative is negative thinking.

Take what you've learned in this book and apply it every day you're alive, with everyone you meet, everywhere you go. Add to your will that you'd like to be buried with this book in case the great beyond doesn't have a great library.

It doesn't matter how many positive thinkers you encounter in a day. All the people you meet who hope you "have a great day" won't necessarily make your day great. That said, I'd like to be the first to say to you today, "Have a negative day!" Your journey to find happiness through negative thinking now continues until the bitter end.

Negativity Scale Checkpoint

Chapter 36: The Bitter End

1. My opinion of death is it's going to be...

   a) Heaven _____ (5 Points)
   b) Short lived _____ (10 Points)
   c) Inconvenient since I don't even rest in peace when I nap or sleep _____ (15 Points)
   d) Hell _____ (20 Points)

2. If I could be granted one wish upon my death, I'd want it to be...

   a) World peace _____ (5 Points)
   b) Reincarnation _____ (10 Points)
   c) A venting session with my maker _____ (15 Points)
   d) The right to take one person of my choice with me _____ (20 Points)

3. When I'm gone, I suspect more people will...

   a) Miss me _____ (5 Points)
   b) Pretend to be me _____ (10 Points)
   c) Slander me _____ (15 Points)
   d) Curse me _____ (20 Points)

4. Having read this book from cover to cover, I believe I will find happiness by living...

   a) The same as I always have _____ (5 Points)
   b) Less positively _____ (10 Points)
   c) In denial _____ (15 Points)
   d) Negatively ever after _____ (20 Points)

5. **Compared to the universe's composition of 95 percent dark energy and dark matter, my body is closer to...**

   a) One hundred percent light energy
      and zero percent dark matter   _____ (5 Points)
   b) Fifty percent light energy and
      fifty percent dark matter   _____ (10 Points)
   c) One hundred percent dark energy
      and zero percent light matter   _____ (15 Points)
   d) It's not light or dark; it's
      psychedelic, man   _____ (20 Points)

Total Points, Chapter 36   _____

In the lost and found of life,
it's easier to find a lost cause.

YOUR NEGATIVITY SCALE SCORE

Up to 250 Points: The Overly Overoptimistic Optimist
More positivity flows through your veins than plasma. You'd feel right at home at a yes-man or yes-woman convention. You're so over-the-top positive that lesser optimists run from you. You are exceedingly agreeable. Poodles can't resist barking, "Nah, nah, ne nah, nah!" at you. You've bought into positivity propaganda for so long, you can't see how vulnerable you are to optimism without realism. You need to reread this book until you can recite everything in it verbatim without looking.

251 to 350 Points: The Humpty Dumpty Thumbs-Upty
You're a wall sitter and a butt squirmer. You'll wait as long as it takes for a positive outcome. When you fall you crack like an egg and slowly leak. You can put yourself back together again; however, you're only setting yourself up for the next fall. You want a fairy tale life but can't go crying to Mommy Goose every time a positive vibe goes bad. Do you hope to get over more humpty and suffer less dumpty? Not sitting on a wall, you won't. Build on something with no ceiling—negativity.

351 to 525 Points: The Swiss-Head-Spinning Equivocator
Your head must feel like it's on a swivel. You circle back and forth between positive and negative so often it would be a miracle if you didn't suffer from eyerollyosis. The holes in your indecisiveness make Swiss cheese look whole. One minute you fondue; the next you fondon't. You stay

neutral like Switzerland but frequently climb a mountain and yodel for help. Stop acting like a Saint Bernard running around chasing its tail. Yodelayheehoo your tail fully over to the negative side.

526 to 600 Points: The Negative Cruise Controller
You're in the sweet spot where negativity comes naturally. You've tasted happiness from negative thinking, and now you're ready for a buffet. Optimists don't understand how you do it. Pessimists envy you. World leaders will soon bow down and kiss your feet. Well, maybe not the last one. You're running on negative autopilot. Be careful not to take it for granted. If you start to become arrogant or rude with your proficiency for negativity, you'll need to move to Boca Raton.

Over 600 Points: The Incredible Sulk
Your capacity for absorbing negative energy is superhuman. When stressed you're capable of going on a rampage that sends everyone running. If you ran into yourself on the street, you'd even get spooked. You seek solitude, but driving people away isn't the way to achieve it. You'd get the same results with body odor. Work on keeping your negative urges and inclinations in check before you need a physicist to genetically reengineer your DNA.

HANDY NEGATIVE TERMS

Absolutely not	If only…	Not a chance
Anything but that	I'll pass	Not now
Bad idea	I'm against it	Nothing I can do
Better than me	I'm beyond help	Run!
Count me out	I'm not buying it	This is stupid, but
Can I go now?	I'm not optimistic	This sucks!
Does it matter?	I'm not sure	That's a problem
Don't bet on it	It won't end well	There's no hope
Don't worry? Ha!	It'll get worse	That's not for me
Dumb idea	It'll never work	That's not right
Forget it	It's a goner	That's terrible

Get someone else	It's a lost cause	That's trouble
Go away	It's beyond me	Time to bail
How annoying	It's boring	Ugh!
I deserved that	It's highly unlikely	Unfortunately, no
I disagree	It's no use	Under water again
I don't believe it	It's not fair	When will I learn?
I don't do that	It's not nothing	When can I leave?
I expected it	It's not my day	We're doomed
I feel like a piñata	It's not worth it	We're screwed
I give in	Just my luck	What's the point?
I knew it	Mayday! Mayday!	What's the use
I never win	Never again	What's wrong?
I screwed up again	No can do	Who cares?
I sense disaster	No expectations	Who will notice?
I want out	No, no, no	Why bother?
I'd be useless	Nokie dokie	Why me?

The appendix has been removed
for fear the book might burst.

ACKNOWLEDGMENTS

Special thanks to the following for making life bearable:

Two-ply toilet paper, naps,
noise-canceling headphones,
and antacid.

ABOUT THE AUTHOR

Larry Gotterer is a negatist and humorist. After experiencing countless disappointments, false hopes, letdowns, and unfulfilled expectations resulting from the positive-driven views of optimists, he discovered the joys of negativity.

Early on Larry's parents encouraged him to be a doctor, and he kind of went into the medical field, but as a patient. He then aspired to be a professor of pessimism; however, he never saw that degree or position offered anywhere. Ultimately his career generated a combination of significant rejection and success as a television producer, writer, and creative consultant as well as a creative director and senior copywriter for advertising and digital marketing agencies.

He lives in God's waiting room, also known as Florida, where the sun shines on his sunscreen-protected, balding head and happy, negative life. He hopes everyone he touches with this book can also find happiness through negative thinking and thanks you for letting him touch you.

REFERENCES

[1] Kristal, Mark B. "Placenta: To Eat or Not to Eat?" HuffPost, November 17, 2012.
https://www.huffpost.com/entry/placenta-to-eat-or-not-to_b_1865446

[2] "'Raisins,' Not 'Virgins,' Quran Scholars Say." Inquirer.net, January 27, 2018.
https://globalnation.inquirer.net/163694/raisins-not-virgins-quran-scholars-say

[3] "Motor Vehicle Injury." Centers for Disease Control and Prevention, October 4, 2019.
https://www.cdc.gov/publichealthgateway/didyouknow/topic/vehicle.html

[4] Knowles, Elizabeth. "What Are Your Chances of Finding a Four-Leaf Clover?" The Science Explorer, March 17, 2016.
http://thescienceexplorer.com/nature/what-are-your-chances-finding-four-leaf-clover

[5] "Most Leaves on a Clover." Guinness World Records, May 10, 2009.
https://www.guinnessworldrecords.com/world-records/most-leaves-on-a-clover

[6] *Horse Feathers*. Film, 1932.

[7] "Feelings by Morris Albert." Songfacts, n.d.
https://www.songfacts.com/facts/morris-albert/feelings

[8] Hendry, Erica R. "7 Epic Fails Brought to You by the Genius Mind of Thomas Edison." Smithsonian Magazine. Smithsonian Institution, November 20, 2013.
https://www.smithsonianmag.com/innovation/7-epic-fails-brought-to-you-by-the-genius-mind-of-thomas-edison-180947786

[9] "Definition of Worry." Lexico. Oxford English Dictionary, n.d. https://www.lexico.com/definition/worry

[10] Goewey, Don Joseph. "85 Percent of What We Worry about Never Happens." HuffPost, December 6, 2017. https://www.huffpost.com/entry/85-of-what-we-worry-about_b_8028368

[11] Enten, Harry. "Congress' Approval Rating Hasn't Hit 30% in 10 Years. That's a Record." CNN politics, June 1, 2019. https://www.cnn.com/2019/06/01/politics/poll-of-the-week-congress-approval-rating/index.html

[12] Tom Petty and the Heartbreakers. *The Waiting. Hard Promises*, 1981. The Rolling Stones, *Time Waits for No One. It's Only Rock 'n Roll,* 1974.

[13] *Network*, United States: MGM, 1976.

[14] Blazer, Christie. "Strategies for Reducing Math Anxiety. Information Capsule. Volume 1102." ERIC. Miami-Dade County Public Schools, August 31, 2011. https://eric.ed.gov/?id=ED536509

[15] Google. Accessed January 11, 2021.

[16] Bártolo, Carolina. "Murphy's Law and Everything That Went Wrong." Medium. Angry Thoughts, October 19, 2017. https://medium.com/angry-channel/murphys-law-and-everything-that-went-wrong-b73b5dfcf0ac.

[17] Schultz, David. "Cheer up! Optimists Live Longer." AAAS, August 26, 2019. https://www.sciencemag.org/news/2019/08/cheer-optimists-live-longer

[18] Sirois, Fuschia. "The Surprising Benefits of Being a Pessimist." The Conversation, February 23, 2018. https://theconversation.com/the-surprising-benefits-of-being-a-pessimist-91851

Norem, Julie K., and Chang, Edward C. "The Positive Psychology of Negative Thinking." Wiley Online Library. John Wiley & Sons, Ltd, August 19, 2002. https://onlinelibrary.wiley.com/doi/abs/10.1002/jclp.10094

[19] "Dark Energy, Dark Matter." NASA Science. NASA, n.d. https://science.nasa.gov/astrophysics/focus-areas/what-is-dark-energy

MENTAL NOTES

LOW NOTES

HIGH NOTES

SIDE NOTES

SWEET NOTES

SOUR NOTES

FALSE NOTES

END NOTES

FINAL NOTES

Made in the USA
Las Vegas, NV
08 April 2021